BRADFORD AT WORK

PEOPLE AND INDUSTRIES THROUGH THE YEARS

PAUL CHRYSTAL

AMBERLEY

ACKNOWLEDGEMENTS

A number of the photographs and images in this book have been made available by various individuals and organisations. The book would be considerably diminished without their kindness and so it gives me pleasure to thank Dave Shaw and Pamela Reynolds, Saltaire History Club, for allowing me to use images published in the *Saltaire Village Society Journal*; Margaret Silver and Simon Palmer for permission to use the Simon Palmer watercolours published in Jim Greenhalf's *Salt & Silver*; and Linda Wilkinson, Salts Mill. Some of the Saltaire images appear in my *Old Saltaire and Shipley* (2014).

A Bradford knocker-upper – early alarm clock technology. Of course, the question on everyone's lips is, 'Who knocks up the knocker?'

First published 2018

Amberley Publishing
The Hill, Stroud
Gloucestershire, GL5 4EP

www.amberley-books.com

Copyright © Paul Chrystal, 2018

The right of Paul Chrystal to be identified as the Author of this work has been asserted in accordance with the Copyrights, Designs and Patents Act 1988.

ISBN 978 1 4456 7150 5 (print)
ISBN 978 1 4456 7151 2 (ebook)

British Library Cataloguing in Publication Data. A catalogue record for this book is available from the British Library.

Origination by Amberley Publishing.
Printed in the UK.

CONTENTS

ABOUT THE AUTHOR

Paul Chrystal was educated at the universities of Hull and Southampton where he took degrees in Classics. He has worked in medical publishing for over thirty-five years, but now combines this with writing features for national newspapers as well as advising visitor attractions such as the National Trust's 'Goddards', the York home of Noel Terry, and 'York's Chocolate Story'. He appears regularly on BBC local radio, on the BBC World Service and on Radio 4's PM programme. He is the author of more than a hundred books on a wide range of subjects, including a number of social histories of various towns and cities in Yorkshire, and aspects of classical history. He is married with three children and lives in Haxby, near York. paul.chrystal@btinternet.com

BY THE SAME AUTHOR

Old Saltaire and Shipley
Leeds in 50 Buildings
Leeds's Military Legacy
Yorkshire Place Names
Huddersfield Through Time
The Confectionery Industry in Yorkshire
Yorkshire Literary Landscapes
Yorkshire Murders

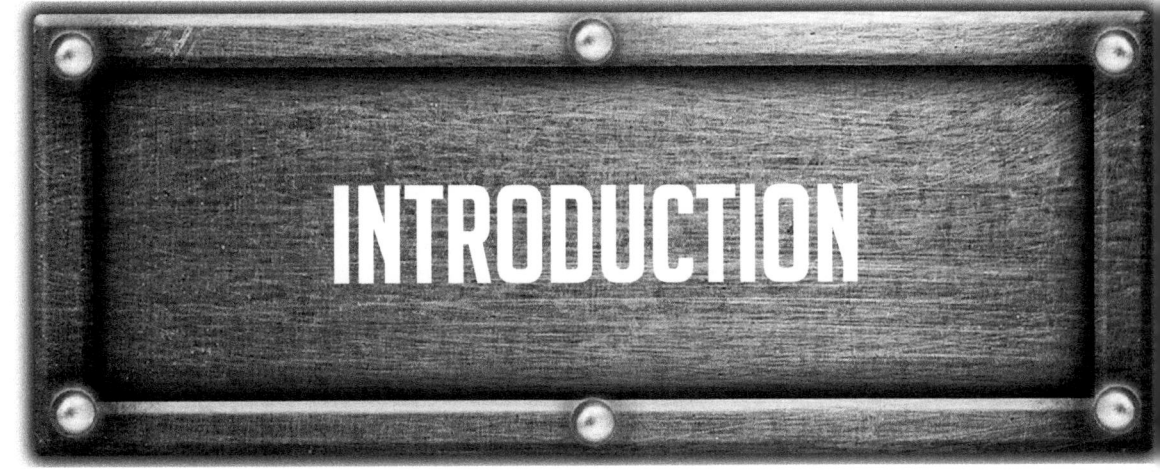

INTRODUCTION

Bradford, or at least industrial Bradford, is defined by mills, ironworks, mines and textiles. Industry first came to life here around 1316 with a fulling mill, a soke mill to mill the local corn, and a market. Within the soke, which extended for a 2-mile radius from Queen's Mill near the centre of Bradford, farmers were obliged to take their corn to the soke mill rather than being allowed to grind it themselves or take it anywhere else. This, of course, made Bradford agronomically very powerful and sowed the seeds for later pre-eminence. Edward IV (r. 1461–83) gave the town the right to hold two annual fairs, which led to increasing commercial prosperity. Henry VIII's reign (r. 1509–47) saw Bradford exceed Leeds as a manufacturing centre and the start of inexorable growth of Bradford over the next 200 years to become the UK's premier wool trade town. In the eighteenth century the Bradford Canal (1774) and turnpike road links boosted trade and industry further; the canal ran the 3 miles from the city centre to join the Leeds & Liverpool Canal at Windhill. Although traffic had diminished by 1894, coal was still being shipped into the city in the 1930s, as the photograph on the next page shows. The end of the nineteenth century saw the completion of the Bradford Midland station (1896).

Portable hand-operated spinning frames and the scribbling machine were introduced toward the end of the latter part of the eighteenth century, substantially increasing productivity. The scribbling machine did the work of several hand operatives and was well suited, like the fulling mill, to be driven from a waterwheel.

The worsted trades grew rapidly in the nineteenth century and while the waterwheel was sufficient to cope with the demands of the early worsted spinning mills, the use of the steam engine in the textile industry was nothing short of revolutionary. The patent on the rotative steam engine held by Boulton and Watt expired in 1800, opening the door for local firms to build and develop bigger, more efficient and cheaper engines to power increasingly larger spinning mills. Power looms had been introduced into the Bradford area by 1822. By 1842, the development of Lister's machine combs coincided with the birth of large textile factories performing all operations under one roof. The old watermills with their limited power were in decline.

With wool playing such an important role in the town, it may not be so surprising that Bradford's substantial cotton industry is often overlooked. We examine the place of cotton in Bradford and the surrounding area, overshadowed even though it was by wool and worsted.

Bradford Canal in around 1935. Canal transportation transformed the Bradford economy.

Bradford Midland station in 1919. This station opened in 1896 with six platforms.

As in other parts of the country, industrial and social unrest erupted from time to time. 1837 saw serious anti-Poor Law riots with operatives clashing with the 15th Hussars; when the Chartists drilled on Fairweather Green in 1839 they caused a riot. In 1842 there were plug-drawing riots (the 1842 General Strike) when Chartists mobilised resistance to wage cuts in the mills, spreading to involve nearly half a million workers throughout Britain and turning into the biggest single demonstration of working-class strength in the nineteenth century. The year 1844 saw Orange disturbances with five protestors charged with manslaughter. On 29 May 1848 the new mayor was forced to call out the dragoons, police and special constables to suppress more Chartist agitation, which led to many injuries. Bradford was 'in a state of siege'.

Reading the 1801 census, Bradford could still be described as a rural market town, with a population of 6,393 cottage industries prevailed with wool spinning and cloth weaving

A 120-spindle flyer spinner built by Smith & Sons, Keighley.

operating in local cottages and farms. Locally, Bradford was little bigger than Keighley (5,745) and smaller than Halifax (8,866) and Huddersfield (7,268). Green grass and countryside still separated Bradford, Manningham, Bowling and Great and Little Horton.

Ironworks at Low Moor and Bowling mark the birth of Bradford as an industrial town from the end of the eighteenth century. They brought with them not just prosperity and employment, but also dramatic population growth and horrific levels of pollution. The Bradford Iron Age overlapped with the textile age in which numerous mills were constructed to produce copious wool worsted products, elevating the town to the status of wool capital of the world.

A significant element of this is attributable to the mill at Saltaire built by Titus Salt, a prominent Bradford mill owner who decamped to a site 4 miles north of the centre of Bradford. He named this Saltaire and constructed his famous industrial village on the doorstep.

Iron, coal and wool constituted the bedrock that underlies the rise of Bradford as an industrial power in the north of England. These strata, of course, were supported by ancillary industries that mushroomed in and around the mills, the mines and the iron plants. In addition, Bradford, like any other town, was provisioned and clothed by various stores, shops, markets and what we might call pop-up smallholdings during the wars. In Bradford's specific case, there were also significant motor car and motorcycle industries – Jowetts and Scotts – which exploited global markets and won international reputations for quality and innovation.

Industry, of course, can never be just about factories, machinery, profit and loss. Without people – workers and owners – there is no industry. As we progress with the story of Bradford's industrial past we inevitably meet these people, and certain themes begin to emerge.

![View of the Great Chartist Meeting on Kennington Common]

William Edward Kilburn (1818–91), *View of the Great Chartist Meeting on Kennington Common* (1848). It was purchased by Prince Albert and is one of a pair of daguerreotypes of the Chartist meeting.

The Morning Wash   Bradfords Back to the Land "pioneers"

'The Morning Wash' – Bradford's Back-to-the-Land pioneers during the First World War. The various Back-to-the-Land movements encouraged people to take up smallholdings to grow food from the land on a small-scale basis, either for themselves or for third parties.

The manifold effects of pollution and of working with hazardous materials on workers' health and life expectancy, the exploitation of children in the workforce, the impact of immigration, industrial unrest, living conditions and community, and lack of accountability among owners and the inevitability of workplace disasters come up time and time again; these essential issues are addressed in the book.

LOW MOOR IRONWORKS

Things started to change dramatically around Bradford in approximated 1788. Before then, Low Moor, 3 miles south of Bradford, was nothing more than a hamlet supporting a handful of cottages in which handloom weavers toiled away, selling their produce in Halifax Piece Hall and similar places. That was before Low Moor Ironworks and its wrought-iron foundries were established and expanded rapidly to become a global name in the production and export of wrought iron and its products from 1801 until 1957. Low Moor was one of five principal steelworks in Bradford, the others being Emmetts (1782), Bowling (1788), Shelf (1792) and Bierley (1811).

Low Moor systematically exploited the high-quality iron ore and low-sulphur coal found locally. The 'better bed' coal was mined from a seam around 18 to 28 inches thick resting on hard sandstone. Around 120 feet above this seam there was a layer of 'black bed' coal, above which was the ironstone holding around 32 per cent iron. The 'Halifax' coal beds lay around 700 feet below the better bed. Recent technological advances made it practical to smelt iron using coal rather than charcoal and to use steam engines in the production of iron goods.

The ironworks in the early 1900s. The carts in the centre were pulled by horses.

The bulk of the ironworks was located on the Royds Hall estate and we have evidence of a coal mine there in 1673. The coal mine potential was developed from 1744 when the owner, Edward Rookes Leeds, began to work the coal mines. From 1780 a wooden railway served the Low Moor mines with lines to the coal yard in Bradford centre, from where the coal was transported on the Leeds & Liverpool Canal. When Mr Leeds went bankrupt the property failed to sell by auction in December 1786 and October 1787. Leeds committed suicide.

In 1788 the estate was sold to a consortium made up of Richard Hird, a country squire, John Preston and John Jarratt for £34,000. The partners in the new enterprise were Hird, Joseph Dawson, a minister, and John Hardy, a solicitor. Dawson had an interest in metallurgy and chemistry and happened to be a close friend of Dr Joseph Priestley. He seems to have been the prime mover in the enterprise.

Work on the construction of the plant began in June 1790, with blast furnaces and casting shops. The two furnaces were blown in on 13 August 1791 and the first casting was made by the forge men three days later on 16 August. First off the production line were domestic goods, soon followed by industrial products such as steam engine components. A major coup came in 1795 when the company won military contracts to provide guns, shot and shells to the government as materiel for the wars with France. By 1799 the works were turning out around 2,000 tons of pig iron per year, from which came a whole range of iron goods from columns used in mill construction to garden furniture.

Wrought-iron products came along in 1801; imported iron was displaced in 1803 by local Low Moor pig iron. Mechanisation continued apace and in 1805 Low Moor could boast a self-tipping inclined railway to charge the furnaces, a nail-slitting mill, two nose-helve hammers and a plate-rolling mill. Philanthropy by the owners included workers' cottages at North Bierley and a hostel for the boys who worked in the pits. These boys were given free clothing and schooling. Several company public houses slaked the thirst of their older colleagues.

By the end of hostilities with France in 1814 the works were producing 33 tons of pig iron every week. Demand, of course, now slumped and prices fell, but military orders were compensated by demand for gas pipes and street lights in 1822.

The Low Moor Co. employed 1,500 men in 1929. With it, over time, came the essential infrastructure and amenities necessary to support a mushrooming population: housing, churches, shops, pubs and public buildings. At one time it was the largest ironworks in Yorkshire, a major complex of mines, mountains of coal and ore, kilns, blast furnaces, forges and slag heaps all connected by a network of railway lines. All of this, of course, came at a price: the surrounding environment was a hell hole of waste, and toxic smoke from the furnaces and kilns blotted out the sun. In 1829 local poet John Nicholson captured the industrial landscape in verse:

When first the shapeless sable ore Is laid in heaps around Low Moor, The roaring blast, the quiv'ring flame, Give to the mass another name: White as the sun the metal runs, For horse-shoe nails, or thund'ring guns ... No pen can write, no mind can soar To tell the wonders of Low Moor.

Orders continued to roll in and in 1835 space was needed for expansion; construction started on a new site to the south-east, where two oven-topped blast furnaces (1836) and a new roll mill to roll iron plate for engine boilers (1842) were installed. The next year, four pairs of forge hammers were installed, driven by steam engines, and in 1844 the company inaugurated one of the newly invented James Nasmyth steam hammers.

The Low Moor Co. purchased the Bierley Ironworks in 1854; by the following year it was producing 21,840 tons of iron per year, and was the largest ironworks in Yorkshire,

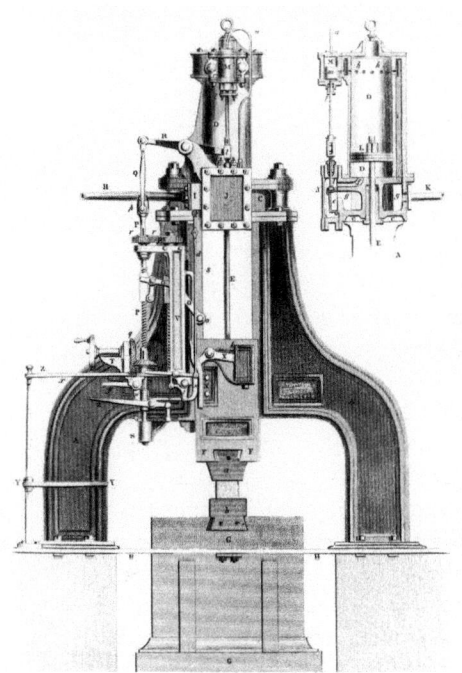

Diagram of a steam hammer patented by Scottish engineer James Nasmyth (1808–90). The illustration is found in *Cyclopædia of Useful Arts, Mechanical and Chemical, Manufactures, Mining, and Engineering*, ed. Charles Tomlinson (London, 1854).

Finished products included guns, shells and shot for troops in the Crimean War (1853–56) and the Indian Mutiny (1857–58), although the arms business suffered when the government increasingly assumed direct control of weapons production. Losses here were compensated by manufacturing weldless railway tyres, steam engine boilers, sugar pans for refineries in the West Indies, water pipes and heavy industry iron components. Pollution was getting worse:

> The natural effect of the perpetual smoke-canopy under which the vegetation of the district exists is to give to it a dinginess not pleasant to look upon... The appearance created by the works themselves and their surroundings has been not inaptly likened to that in the vicinity of the crater of some volcano.
>
> William Cudworth, *Round about Bradford* (1876)

By 1863 there were 3,600 employees, including 1,993 miners, 420 furnacemen, 770 forgemen and 323 engineers. In 1864 and 1871 additional steam hammers were bought and new rolling mills were built to provide iron plates for shipbuilding. By 1867 there were around 4,000 employees.

In 1868 Low Moor ironstone peaked when 617,628 tons of Low Moor ironstone were raised. There were 2,000 coal miners in 1876 toiling in pits ranging in depth from 30 to 150 yards in surrounding North Bierley, Tong, Bowling, Shelf, Wyke, Clifton, Hipperholme and Cleckheaton and a further 800 miners in collieries to the east at Beeston, Churwell, Osmondthorpe and Potternewton, near Leeds. Thirteen pumping engines drained water from the mines. Low Moor iron was prized for its quality and commanded premium prices.

Things started to go wrong, though, in the late 1880s. With its mines increasingly scattered and expensive to run, the rail network operating on a variety of gauges with an uneconomic mix of stationary engines and locomotives, obsolete plant and inefficient operations, the slide had begun. Two new blast furnaces at the New Works failed to save the company; other attempts to restore success included an electrical power station in 1905 with boilers fired by

Low Moor – note the proximity of housing in both photographs.

Low Moor.

gas from the blast furnaces, and electrical drives replaced steam drives. The First World War saw a temporary surge in demand for shell casings and drop forgings, including shoes for the tracks of the first military tanks.

After the war, various attempts were made to cut costs, but these had a deleterious effect on quality. In 1928 the company was declared bankrupt, and the Low Moor assets were bought by Thos. W. Ward Ltd. In 1971 new owners were producing alloy steel, making around 350 tons per week.

THE 1916 LOW MOOR EXPLOSION

On 21 August 1916 one of the UK's worst industrial disasters took place. It was at Low Moor Munitions Co. ('Factory No. 182, Yorkshire'), the Low Moor Chemical Co. before the war, at the bottom of New Works Road, where large amounts of picric acid, a constituent used in the making of high explosives, was being manufactured. Also known as lyddite – after Lydd, in

Debris and detritus following the explosion. This was the railway signal box.

Kent, where the initial acceptance trials were made – the acid also comes in yellow dye form and is used in the manufacture of carpets.

On that fateful day, the factory housed 30,000 lb of picric acid, which was awaiting tests and then shipment. More still was being processed and in transit from the drying sheds to the lower magazine. At 2.30 p.m. a worker was moving picric acid across the yard when he heard a hissing sound; there was no fire alarm, the water sprinklers were on but no one could remember if any water was ever sprinkled. What everyone did know was that a huge explosion was imminent.

Ten minutes later that explosion came, sending up a fireball. It was heard as far away as York some 40 miles away. Debris rained down all around and the smell of bad eggs filled the air.

Despite the valiant efforts of the works fire brigade to bring the resulting inferno under control, the fire continued unrestrained. When the first of the Bradford firemen arrived from Odsal station, joined later by eighteen men from Central, a huge explosion blew them completely off the engine and, in the words of Chief Officer Scott, 'within half an hour of turning out to the fire, all eighteen men were in the infirmary or killed'. The Odsal engine was crushed under a wall, killing two firemen.

Further explosions, large and minor, kept coming, scattering blazing debris all over the place, and soon the whole works were destroyed. At nearby North Bierley Works in Cleckheaton Road, a large gasometer containing 270,000 cubic feet (7,600 m3) of gas was ruptured by cascading debris. The escaping gas soon ignited; the exploding heat was felt almost a mile away and the noise rendered one seven-year-oldboy deaf. Wartime censorship ensured that no mention of the disaster was reported by the press.

In the railway sidings almost thirty carriages and wagons were destroyed and 100 others seriously damaged. Casualties were rushed to hospital in handcarts. The explosions continued

The gasometer before it blew up.

for two days; it was three days before the fire was extinguished completely. People had to stay with friends and family, and some slept in woods or sheltered in schools. Three schools were forced to close. Houses and shops within a 2-mile radius had their windows smashed and roofs damaged, ceilings caved in and doors destroyed. Some properties were totally demolished by the explosion and twenty-nine houses in First Street were built in 1919 as replacements. Terrified dogs fled the scene, some later found as far away as Wakefield, Huddersfield and Halifax. Thirty-four people were killed and sixty injured in the works. Outside the works, many more were injured by flying shards of glass and debris.

THE BOWLING IRONWORKS

The Bowling Iron Works was an ironworking complex established around 1780 in East Bowling, to the south-east of central Bradford. Bowling township lay above the Yorkshire coalfield where, in the eighteenth and nineteenth centuries, deposits of black bed and better bed coal were prolific – these deposits were good for coke; there was also substantial deposits of limestone. All were near the surface, facilitating extraction. The Bowling Iron Works operation included mining coal and iron ore, smelting, refining, casting and forging. The company turned out shackles, hooks and piston rods for locomotives, colliery cages and other mining appliances where tough iron was a prerequisite.

Surface coal was being extracted from outcrops and shallow pits as early as 1360; we have records of coal mines being worked by 1502. As with Low Moor, the ironstone yielded around 32 per cent iron. Better bed coal is free of sulphur, making it ideal for furnaces used in smelting, puddling and forging. The black bed coal, nearer to the surface, could be sold or used for firing boilers and other purposes.

Mining began on Jeremiah Rawson's estate, then extended into nearby estates as the deposits became exhausted, always mining the same beds of minerals. The first foundry was established around 1788 by a group of experienced mining businessmen including John Sturges, an ironmaster with works at Fall Ing Works at Wakefield, and Richard Paley, an iron merchant of Leeds. Iron was initially shipped into the foundry from Wakefield. Finished products at this time were largely domestic; for example, cast-iron grates, laundry irons, ovens, boilers, frying pans, window sash weights and clock weights. A smelting plant was in operation in 1788, producing pig iron that was used in the boiler plates for the first steam engine at the Low Moor works.

Bowling could boast some of the earliest machine shops in the country, complete with travelling cranes and cutting-edge machinery for turning, drilling, boring and fitting. There were two hammer shops including one early state-of-the-art Nasmyth hammer. An extensive tramway system connected departments and facilitated the movement of raw materials, thus minimising haulage costs. This 22-mile internal system was linked by a small branch line to the Great Northern Railway.

The Bowling works were contracted to provide large quantities of guns including howitzers and carronades (a short large-calibre cannon), shot and shells to the British government before 1790.

Above: An old carronade, part of a now neglected display in the archway of the old clock tower of the Carron Works, near Falkirk. (Photo by Kim Traynor)

Left: A female worker demonstrates a lifting device for barrels at the Bowling Iron Works in November 1918. (Imperial War Museum)

Before the invention of wrought iron, cast iron was used for guns, subject to rigorous production controls and quality tests. When Sir William Armstrong invented wrought-iron guns, some of the first coils he used were made from Bowling iron.

By the 1848 iron production in Yorkshire stood at 66,650 tons with Bowling one of the major producers. One of their specialties – reflecting the local pre-eminence in the textile industry – was the production of steam presses.

A female worker demonstrates a machine that can lift boxes at the Bowling Iron Works, Bradford, in November 1918. (Imperial War Museum)

Another female worker demonstrating the same, November 1918. (Imperial War Museum)

INDUSTRIAL POLLUTION

As with Low Moor, all this industrial activity did little for local aesthetics or environmental health: an 1876 description was reminiscent of Virgil's description of Lake Acheron, the entrance to the Underworld, Hell, in *Aeneid* Book 6:

On the right is a large waste space, with the steaming lake and cinder hills behind. At night, when live scoria and ashes glow from the sides of the latter, and the lake is lighted up by vivid and fitful gleams emitted from the blast furnaces, the scene is strange and weird-like ... one might almost fancy himself in immediate proximity to an active volcano.

The Bowling Iron Co., then, made a significant contribution to Bradford's reputation as one of Britain's most polluted towns. The issue was researched by Clement Richardson and reported in *The Bradford Antiquary*, the journal of the Bradford Historical and Antiquarian Society, in 1986 in volume 2, pp. 28 – 34 in an article entitled 'Clearing the Air'. In his introduction, Richardson states:

Not so long ago the image of Bradford was one of blackened buildings shrouded in the smoke of countless mill chimneys, and this view may persist with those unfamiliar with the present-day smokeless city. Bradford was the archetypal 'coaltown', the product of 19th century industrialisation. That it was built on coal is true both in the literal and the

A part of the ironworks.

Another part of the ironworks in 1861.

metaphorical sense. Its rich, accessible and varied deposits of coal, iron ore, and other useful minerals were the main sources of its phenomenal growth in the last century [the twentieth]. However, by 1840 the town had acquired an unflattering reputation as one of the smokiest places in Britain. It took almost 130 years to clean up its atmosphere, during which time the inhabitants paid a high price in pulmonary deaths and environmental squalor.

Richardson then goes on to show how there was a noticeable fall in mortality in the city following the 1926 coal strike, when more effective national legislation was introduced to reduce atmospheric smoke and after which there was a reduced level of industrial activity during the 1930s slump. He demonstrates how 'reduction in smoke was matched by a fall in the number of deaths from chest ailments, providing strong evidence to support the views of a succession of local medical officers that there was a causal link between air pollution and respiratory disorders'.

In 1803 the Bradford Improvement Act decreed that, 'Engine chimneys are to be erected of sufficient height as not to create a nuisance by the emission of smoke. All owners of engines etc. are to construct fireplaces thereof in such a manner as most effectually to destroy and consume the smoke arising there from.'

Local byelaws ordained that a chimney height of at least 90 feet be mandatory and that there be restricted smoke emissions. With no wind, especially in winter, polluted air was trapped in the basin-shaped valley of the Bradford Beck, giving rise to fatal 'pea-soupers'. The prescribed high mill chimneys in theory helped to discharge gases and smoke into the upper air to be dispersed by the turbulence up there. The council's byelaws were largely ignored and smoke nuisance inspectors reported regular violations where mill chimneys were below the required height, or where mill owners neglected to fit smoke-burning equipment.

Bradford Beck ('T' Mucky Beck') flows through Bradford and on to the River Aire at Shipley. It was built over in the nineteenth century so that as it reaches Bradford city centre it runs underground. It is culverted from Bradford city centre to Queen's Road, after which it runs mostly in an open channel to Shipley. The culverts were constructed to hide the sight and smells of the river from the Bradford population. Bradford Beck was known as the filthiest river in England.

In 1841 it was said, 'The condition of Bradford is dreadful. Lowmoor iron-forges most extensively spread their suffocating exhalations on the one side ... On the other side, Bowling Iron Hell (for it is one truly) casts a still denser atmosphere and sulphurous stench...' The council's lame response to the numerous breaches of the byelaws was, in 1867, 'that the problem be tackled in a spirit of conciliation'.

Part of the problem, apart from profit and greed, was the general consensus that the factories provided work, so should not be pressured into reducing pollution. This was clarified beyond all doubt when in 1884 the Borough Medical Officer, Dr T. W. Hime, 'attributed the lack of effective remedial action to the widespread belief that because factories provided work, the employers should not be pressed too hard'. He added that the low fines were useless as a deterrent. Interestingly, as Richardson points out, council committee minutes expose how Bradford's leading industrialists were frequent offenders, and some of them had been, or were, council members. In effect the councillors who formulated the byelaws, exercised responsibility for their enforcement and acted as judges when offenders were finally taken to court, were at times the very people who broke the law. Thus in 1875 eight of the thirteen members of the Smoke Prevention Subcommittee were in manufacturing, and one of the remaining five was a coal merchant.

Respiratory diseases were rife, peaking in 1890 during an influenza epidemic. In 1874 the Bowling Iron Company, a persistent offender, was fined £5, with £9 10s costs for ten offences.

John Pickles, the Smoke Nuisance Inspector, had reported in 1867 that he and his assistants visited 264 works and served 683 smoke prevention notices including one on the council's own public baths in 1868. In 1903, 103 notices were served on local owners of steam engines, of which seventy-one cases reached the courts. Of these, forty-nine were fined a pathetic average of 10s with 6 and 8d costs.

Bradford's industrial pollution had been causing some concern since the beginning of the nineteenth century, a time when Bradford had only a few coal-burning steam engines, foundries, and the major ironworks at Bowling, Low Moor and Shelf, together with the steadily belching smoke from a multitude of household fires. The number of steam-driven textile mills increased to eighty-three in 1841 and to 133 in 1871.

The 1867 report of the Smoke Prevention Subcommittee of Bradford Council listed 591 boilers burning 1,200 tons of coal a day, and another 1,300 tons as being consumed in other industrial establishments in the borough. These chimneys belched out large quantities of smoke, ash, sulphur and other irritants into the atmosphere ... there was a rise in deaths from chest diseases between 1860 and 1880.

It might have been hoped that Bradford's incorporation as a borough in 1847 provided an opportunity to clear the town's air. But no records show that, as in 1803, the smoke control byelaws 'were not enforced with sufficient strictness to reduce the smoke and the deaths which occurred through related chest diseases'. This was despite the best efforts of a councillor called Bilton, who, in 1848, moved 'that the 65th byelaw dealing with the consumption of smoke, be carried into effect' and of Titus Salt, a prominent local industrialist and Bradford's second mayor, who recorded in 1853 that it was not for him 'to do anything to pollute the air and water'. Salt had earlier fitted smoke-consuming equipment into his Bradford factories, but his innovative and inspired technology, when offered to others, was snubbed by his fellow mill owners.

Nevertheless, the link between air pollution and respiratory diseases continued to be pressed home by the medical authorities. The town's Medical Officer of Health in 1884 referred to the deleterious effects of a smoke-filled atmosphere in 'excluding sunlight, rendering life precarious for man and animals'. His successor, Dr J. McLintock, reported that he was 'inclined to think that our high mortality from chest diseases, including consumption, is in some measure due to the irritation caused by the unnecessarily polluted state of the air which we are obliged to breathe'.

Bradford Medical Officer's reports from 1859 until 1974 illustrate that deaths from respiratory diseases 'were at a rate of 3.50 per 1000 in 1859 and were still running at 4.30 per 1000 at the end of the century. The rates fell from 2.45 in 1900 to 1.37 in 1931, but rose slightly during the post-war trade boom and settled down to 1.52 per 1000 in 1971. By the end of the latter period a clean air programme had been implemented for the whole of the city'.

The glowering smog would not go away. As late as 1930 the average fine, plus costs, for discharging black smoke for more than a total of three minutes in the half hour was £1 6s 11d. It was patently cheaper for firms to pay the fines and costs than to install smoke-eliminating equipment. This kit was described as 'economisers', the irony of which was not lost on Bradford's Medical Officer of Health in 1884: 'when he argued that the large amount of smoke in the atmosphere 'represented a permanent leakage of profits of a very considerable amount. The visible cloud of smoke which hangs over the town is unburnt fuel'.

As might be expected, the similarities of the Bowling Iron Works to Low Moor did not end with their joint contribution to the nation's bronchitis black spot: the plant included blast furnaces and refineries, puddling and ball furnaces with high brick or iron chimneys, a shed housing the steam hammers, steelworks, a large machine shop, boiler works, a large foundry and other workshops and buildings. A narrow-gauge railway moved material within the works, and a line to the Great Northern Railway was used to transport the products. A network of tramways fetched minerals from the pitheads to the works, with wagons pulled by wire ropes powered by stationary engines. Four large pumps helped keep the mines dry.

HUMAN RESOURCES

Drinking the wages was a problem. H. Hartopp, manager of the Bowling Works, tells how

All our colliers and miners are in our direct employ, without the intervention of contractors. They appoint one of their number, the head man in the pit, to come to the office every week to receive the money. It is given to him in sovereigns and silver, perhaps 20l or 30l … There is no need, whatever, that they should go to a public house to divide it, but I believe their practice, too often, is to do so. I have been anxious to put an end to it, by providing them with a convenient room near the collieries, where practicable; but they are scattered and distant.

The company also made efforts to minister to its workers' spiritual and educational needs. Bowling Iron built St John's Church, paid for out of its own pocket for £5,000. It was consecrated on 8 February 1842 and, aptly, was the first to be built in England of iron and stone, with only the rafters made of wood. St John's School in Bowling was less of a philanthropic success: the company had built the building, but did not contribute much financially; there were on average 150 children at the school, of whom only twelve were factory workers; only seven of these children were aged thirteen or older. Poor lighting and ventilation were problems, as was the unavailability of a teacher for the older children.

CHILD LABOUR IN THE MINES

Back in the mines child labour was rife and conditions were dire. Hurrier-boys were hired to drag heavy carriages along tracks to the miners, then drag the even heavier loaded carriages back to the pit shaft and hook them to a chain so they could be pulled up. An 1843 inquiry into child labour reported on one Jabez Scott, aged fifteen, a worker at the Bowling Iron Works: 'Work is very hard; sleeps well sometimes, sometimes is very ill, tired and cannot sleep so well.' An 1847 report noted that there was considerable temptation to employ boys in the mines even though they were below the legal age – then ten years of age. All the managers did was moan: 'Managers, & c., of mines, complain that the work required of boys in seams of coal not more than 18 inches to two feet thick, is done at a disadvantage, unless they are brought to it from their earliest years.'

The year 1875 was a bad one for Bowling: there was a terrible explosion in the company's Crosses Pit mine, where forty men and boys were working. Four ironstone getters and hurriers met their deaths here, and others were injured when gunpowder being used to break up large pieces of scale that contained the ironstone accidentally ignited. At that time Bowling employed around 2,000 workmen in the collieries; deaths through industrial accidents were running at two each year. Accident rates were higher in the ironworks, although employment numbers here were lower. Boys were employed in wheeling hot lumps of puddled iron to the hammers, for example.

The Company went into liquidation in 1898. In 1903 it was reorganised as the Bowling Iron Company, but was finally liquidated in 1921.

Clearer skies over Bradford centre in the early twenty-first century.

THE WOOL CAPITAL OF THE WORLD

The Bradford economy owes as much to its pre-eminence as an international textile hub as it does to iron and steel. Bradford's textile industry can be dated back to the thirteenth century, but 1825 was a pivotal year. That was the year when the wool-combers union called a strike that lasted five-months; workers were eventually forced back to work through penury and the much-dreaded introduction of machine-combing went ahead. This local industrial revolution ushered in a period of rapid growth, with wool imported in prodigious quantities for the manufacture of worsted cloth. Worsted was a fine wool fabric used in top-end clothing and refers to a type of yarn and the fabric produced by this yarn. There are two principal types of wool yarn: woollen and worsted, using fleeces from different breeds of sheep that are prepared and spun differently. Worsted uses fleeces that have long fibres using combing machines to ensure the wool fibres lie parallel to each other and are of the same length. This produces a smooth, strong yarn. In woollen yarn, the fibres are shorter, of varying length, and point in all directions; they are fluffy and uneven.

A Noble comb-spinning machine at Bradford Industrial Museum. (Photograph by Linda Spashett)

A 120-spindle flyer spinner at Bradford Industrial Museum. (Photograph by Linda Spashett)

Spindle rover made in Keighley for Clarence Mills, Halifax, at Bradford Industrial Museum. (Photograph by Linda Spashett)

Right: 100 per cent worsted wool yarn showing the plied structure. (Photograph by Pschemp)

Below: Worsted spinner and spinning mule at Bradford Industrial Museum. (Photograph by Linda Spashett)

Worsted yarn produces fabrics that are durable and have a fine, smooth texture while woollen products are softer and warmer. Worsted yarn is used in clothing such as men's suits and woollen yarns are more suitable for knitwear and blankets. Bradford earned the sobriquet 'Worstedopolis'.

In 1800, Bradford's population was 13,000 and it had just one spinning mill. By 1850, the population had grown to 103,000, while the number of spinning mills had surged to 129. In 1900, the number of mills had increased further to 350. Two-thirds of the country's wool production was now processed in Bradford.

The Warping and Winding department in Goodman, Abbott & Wright in the 1950s.

Bradford coal kept the mills and other industries in power, and local sandstone was mined for building the many mills. By 1850, the population had risen to 182,000, attracting yet more workers to jobs in the textile mills. Local soft water was used in cleaning raw wool but water, or the lack of it, was a seriously restricting problem in Bradford Dale, curbing as it did industrial expansion and the improvement of urban sanitary conditions. So, in 1854 Bradford Corporation bought the Bradford Water Company and initiated a huge engineering programme to deliver soft water from Airedale and Wharfedale. Urban creep took in the Hortons and Bowling, resulting in an interrupted urban and industrial landscape by the late nineteenth century, swallowing up the green fields between each of the communities.

One significant employer was Samuel Lister and his brother, who were worsted spinners and manufacturers at Lister's Mill, or Manningham Mills. Among other things, Lister's could lay claim to over 200 factory chimneys spewing out toxic black, sulphurous smoke all day long, adding to the regular outbreaks of cholera and typhoid. A shocking statistic – even by the standards of the day – is that only 30 per cent of children born to textile workers reached the age of fifteen. Life expectancy in Bradford was just over eighteen years, one of the lowest in the country.

CHILD LABOUR IN THE MILLS

In England and Scotland in 1788, two-thirds of the workers in 143 water-powered cotton mills were children. Children made up a significant proportion of the workforce in Bradford's textile mills: families relied heavily on the extra income the children brought in. Some parents even sold their children to mill owners. Children often worked up to fourteen hours a day. Work roles performed by child workers included the following:

- 'Scavengers' were the smallest and youngest members of the workforce. They crawled about collecting the fibres of wool that fell under the machines – a hazardous task when you think that the deafening and dangerous machines were still running all the while.
- 'Lap joiners' had to keep the spinning machines constantly fed with wool. They swiftly joined together the end of one wool top and the start of the next wool top. Skin sores were common as a result of this work.

Child labour – a global problem. This image shows children working in a mill in Macon, Georgia, in 1909.

- 'Piecers' joined together, by hand, any threads that were broken during spinning and weaving. Broken ends had to be fixed rapidly to ensure the work continued. Speed and dexterity were essential: piecers could easily walk up to 20 miles a day doing their job.

In a bid to curb this ongoing atrocity the Factory Acts were passed. Children younger than nine were not allowed to work; those aged nine to sixteen could work sixteen hours per day as laid down by the Cotton Mills Act. In 1856, the law allowed children over the age of nine to work sixty hours per week, night or day. In 1901, the permitted child labour age was raised to twelve.

LISTER'S MILLS

Lister's Mill, or Manningham Mills, was the largest silk factory in the world. Samuel Cunliffe Lister built it in 1873 in the Italianate style to replace the original Manningham Mills after it was burnt to the ground in 1871.

In its heyday, 11,000 men, women and children were working at Lister's – all busy making top-end textiles such as velvet and silk. In 1911 the firm supplied 1,000 yards of velvet for George V's coronation and in 1976 new velvet curtains for President Ford at the White House.

Lister's was complicit in the formation of the Independent Labour Party with the 1890–91 strike at the mill. When US import tariffs began to impact on the bottom line, Lister's simply and capriciously used the expedient of posting a notice in the mill announcing the intention to cut the wages of 1,100 workers by 25 per cent in the run-up to Christmas, and threatening to lock out those who refused. The shambolic but determined workforce were furious and at its height the strike saw 5,000 workers downing tools from December to April with riots in the streets amid futile attempts to negotiate a settlement.

Isabella Ormston Ford (1855–1924) was mainly active in Leeds, where she worked tirelessly among tailoresses who were campaigning for improved working conditions. She helped Emma

Above: Lister's Mill from the ground.

Below: Lister's Mill from above with a smoking chimney.

Above: Wool sorters taking a break. This mill is now the Treadwell Gallery. Nicholas Treadwell (b. 1937) owns the Nicholas Treadwell Gallery, which started in 1963 inside touring vehicles, after which it was run housed in buildings in London, Bradford and finally Austria. In 1987 Treadwell opened Treadwell's Art Mill for superhumanist work in a three-storey former wool mill in Little Germany, Bradford. The Art Mill provided residency for fourteen artists, as well as a theatre, cinema and a vegetarian café. The current Treadwell Gallery is situated in the former courthouse and prison in the Austrian village of Aigen, north of Linz. (Photograph by Ian Beesley)

Right: The bronze of Isabella Ford in Leeds City Museum.

Patterson, president of the Women's Protective and Provident League, to form a Machinists' Society for female tailors in Leeds – the opening shot in a long campaign by Ford to improve the pay and conditions of women working in the textile industry in West Yorkshire. In 1890 she marched with workers from Manningham Mills. During the 1890s Isabella was active in propaganda work for the ILP all over the West Riding of Yorkshire, speaking 'often at street corners, in dingy club rooms, in hot, crowded school rooms'. (*Bradford Pioneer*, July 1924). She was the author of numerous pamphlets including *Women's Wages* (1893), *Industrial Women and How to Help Them* (1900), and *Women and Socialism* (1904).

Lister, meanwhile, equivocated and dissimulated, threatening to close down the mill altogether and move production to Addingham; he then denounced his workforce in a letter to the local press, exposing his ignorant, arrogant prejudices based on stereotypical views of the working classes and their alleged innate fecklessness: 'The women spend their money on dress and the men on drink, so that the begging box goes round – it matters not what wages are.' Fine words from the great paternalist and philanthropist. His verbal arrogance turned out to be a highly effective recruiting manifesto for the trade unions and for the nascent Independent Labour Party; Lister's workers now rejected the haughty Liberal politicians who had rejected them. A mural at the back of the Bradford Playhouse in Little Germany commemorates the centenary of the founding of the Independent Labour Party (later the Labour Party) in Bradford at the founding conference in January 1893.

Left: Wool bales being loaded.

Below: Legions of Jones sewing machines in action.

The striking workers were denied any help from the poor relief, so it was not long before poverty and hunger drove the strikers back to work in April 1891, giving Lister a complete victory and maintaining his precious profit margins.

When completed in 1873, Lister's Mill was the biggest textile mill in the north of England with a floor space of 27 acres; it still dominates the Bradford skyline. The chimney stands 249 feet high, it cost around £10,000 and its total weight is estimated at 8,000 tons. Samuel Lister proudly called it 'Lister's Pride'.

Lister had invented the Lister nip comb, a tool that separated and straightened raw wool, a necessary task that has to be done before the wool can be spun into worsted yarn – a hot, dirty and tiring job. The nip comb revolutionised the industry. Around 1855 he concentrated on finding a way to use the fibre in silk waste. Finally, and on the verge of bankruptcy, he managed to perfect silk-combing equipment, which enabled him to make high-quality yarn at a low cost. He also invented the velvet loom for piled fabrics.

Until electric power was switched on in 1934, the mill was driven by massive steam boilers that consumed 1,000 tons of coal every week, all shipped in on company rail wagons from company collieries near Pontefract. The company had its own water supply including a large covered reservoir on-site.

Lister's did its bit in the Second World War, turning out 1,330 miles of parachute silk, 284 miles of flame-proof wool, 50 miles of khaki battledress and 4,430 miles of parachute cord.

Foreign competition and changing textile fashions, such as increased use of artificial fibres, did for Lister's and in 1992 the mills closed.

Titus Salt, of whom we shall read more later, was a major Bradford employer. In 1833 he assumed control of his father's woollen business, specialising in exotic fabrics combining alpaca, mohair, cotton and silk. By 1850 he could boast five mills, but Salt was not prepared to put up with the grimy, polluted environment, the squalid living conditions endured by his workers and the serious occupational health hazards they lived, or died, with. Bradford had some of the worst housing and sanitary conditions in the country and one of the lowest life

The Lister and Co. transport fleet lined up and ready to go at Manningham Mills.

Inside the mill.

A Lister comb manufactured by John Perry, Shipley, 1888.

A wonderful shot of a silk spinner spinning in Lister's Mill. (Photograph by Ian Beesley)

expectancies. According to a sanitary commissioner report, 'Taking the general condition of Bradford, I am obliged to pronounce it to be the most filthy town I visited.' (James Smith, 'Report on the Sanatory Condition of the Town of Bradford, Health of Towns Commission, 2nd Report', 1845, Vol. XVIII, Part 2, p.315)

Salt left Bradford behind and transferred his business to Salt's Mill in nearby Saltaire in 1850, where in 1853 he began to build the workers' village, now a UNESCO World Heritage Site.

THE BOWLING DYE WORKS

Bradford products were formerly dyed in Wakefield or Leeds, but it was dyeing its own by 1797 when there were two dye houses working in the town – Bowling Dye Works and Peel's of Thornton Road.

Salt was not the only Bradford industrialist with vision and a degree of compassion. In the 1860s Henry Ripley was managing partner of Edward Ripley & Son Ltd, which owned the Bowling Dye Works, a concern that in 1880 employed over 1,000 people and was reputedly the biggest dye works in Europe. Like Salt he had political clout: he was a councillor, JP and Bradford MP intent on improving working-class housing and working conditions. He too went on to build an industrial model village – Ripley Ville – on a site in Broomfields, East Bowling, near to the dye works. In addition to his income from the dye works income he had revenues rentals from several mills. But Ripley was intent on improving the living conditions of his workers.

Dying was always a highly toxic process, and remains so today, not least in China and India where poisonous polluted water is often released back into the environment. This photo shows the dye house in Salt Mills in 1930, with its toxic fumes and dyes. In Salt's days workers were exposed daily to toxins and their fumes, with no masks or protective clothing. Dye fixatives were especially lethal. They contained dioxin, a carcinogen, heavy metals such as chrome, copper, zinc (also carcinogens), and formaldehyde.

THE DYE WORKS DISASTERS

Fifty-five years before the 1916 Low Moor Munitions Company disaster on 21 June 1861, a boiler exploded at the dye works causing widespread destruction of property and the death of sixty-four-year-old William Rouse, and serious injury to Isaac Brook. The boiler was ripped from its seating, blown in two lengthwise, and the centre part, weighing nearly 4 tons, hurtled high into the air, rolled up like sheet lead, and blasted some 30 yards. The official cause of the accident was that the plate had worn so thin by corrosion that it could no longer bear the pressure.

In 1862 Sir Henry Ripley commissioned a 240-foot-high chimney to be built over an old coal shaft, which was filled with concrete to form a central pillar for the chimney. Recommendations by the local clerk of the works went ignored. Instead there was a brick lining with stone facing and 'backing' of loose rubble between the two. Ornament, all the fashion, was much more important to Ripley than safety and practicalities. There was much kudos to be had from a chimney that passed for a cathedral, country house or Italian villa.

Unfortunately the extra work beautifying the chimney also weakened it, and it was left with a pronounced Pisa-like tilt. Parts of the building were rented out to various firms in the area, including A. Haley & Co., W. H. Greenwood & Co. and J. Horsfall & Co. However, over the next twenty years, repairs had to be carried out regularly to bolster up the chimney, until in 1882 cracks in the wall developed into bulges.

On 20 December Francis Haley, the agent and manager of the mill, wrote to Henry Ripley Jr to register a complaint regarding the state of the chimney, stating that Mr Humphreys, the builder at the mill, 'is of the opinion that the damaged portion which is four or five yards in length, will be forced out before the end of the week'. He was told to stop people walking nearby as an adequate safety measure; no actual remedial work was authorised.

An examination of the inside of the chimney to ascertain the full extent of the problem would have meant allowing it to cool down, and that would have entailed stopping work – not an option. Then some of the outer casing fell off and, on 28 December, after a very windy night, the whole chimney fell directly onto the mill, destroying many of the buildings and killing fifty-four people.

Despite irrefutable evidence that the owners had known of the precarious state of the chimney, a verdict of accidental death was found. It took three days to recover all the bodies.

The following throws much-needed light on the working conditions of the time, of child labour, of health and safety non-accountability on the part of factory owners, and on the cavalier and shabby way in which workers were treated:

James Henderson was the father of two of the girls killed in the accident and in 1884 he took Sir Edward Ripley, Ripley's brothers and a Mr Taylor to court. The case appeared before Justice Manisty and a jury at Leeds summer assizes. Henderson was a wool comber working for Greenwoods, a firm which rented part of Ripley's mill. His two daughters, Mary and Sarah Jane, worked as drawers for the firm of Sugden & Briggs, also in the mill complex. Mary earned 7s 6d a week whilst Sarah Jane was a half-timer, working part of the day in the mill and spending the rest of the day in school, earning 3s 6d, though their colleague James Nicholls told the court that their wages would soon have risen to 11s and 9s respectively. This was an important consideration since most families at the time relied heavily on children's earnings to support the family. Henderson also had five other younger children to look after. The two girls worked from six in the morning to half past five or six at night. After their death the Ripley firm paid their funeral expenses and gave seven weeks' wages as [derisory] compensation.

(Adapted from *Collapse of Newland Mill Chimney in Bowling, Bradford,* by Vivien Teasdale http://www.on-magazine.co.uk/yorkshire/yorkshire-history/collapse-of-newland-mill-chimney-bowling-bradford/accessed, 24 October 2017)

RIPLEY VILLE

The industrial model village grew out of the lamentable conditions in which workers were obliged to toil and live during the Industrial Revolution. The villages were a culmination, generally speaking, of a growing awareness that something had to be done about the overcrowding and the insanitary, disease-ridden houses and squalid streets that droves of workers left each dawn for the inhumane factory conditions and relentless

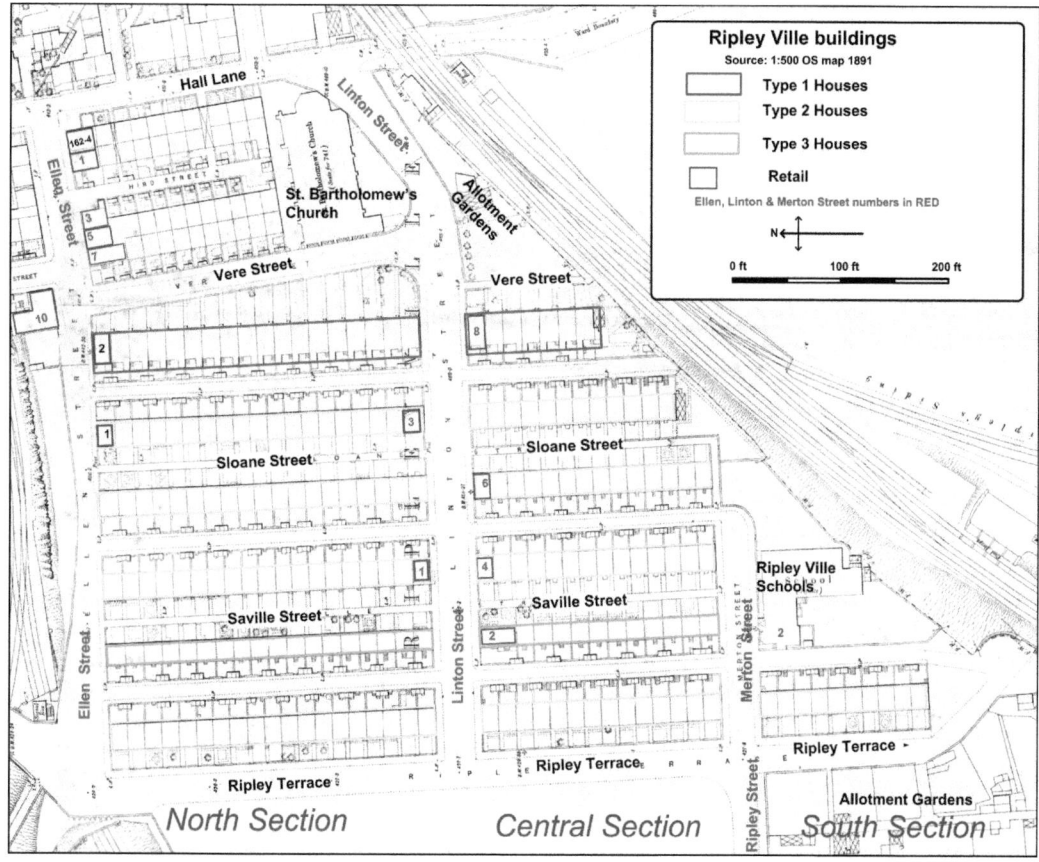

North Section   Central Section   South Section

labour that paid their meagre wages. The industrial village concept, however, was never just a question of altruism, philanthropy or paternalism. The welfare could never exist without the business, and profitable business at that: the difference between the industrialist who built his model village and the average factory owner was that the benefactor felt the need to reinvest his profits for the betterment of his workers while at the same time benefitting from a stable, more productive, comparatively happy workforce.

The serious shortcomings of back-to-back housing – the predominant form of working- class housing for many years – were there for all to see in all industrial towns and cities, and most of the agencies involved agreed that something radical had to be done to stop the proliferation of what were little more than wretched hovels. A bylaw of 1860 theoretically banned construction of back-to-back houses, but, predictably, the building companies rallied together to mount a campaign to rescind the bylaw, their argument being that it was not possible to build 'through' houses at a price that working-class people could afford. Politics intervened when in the local elections of 1865 the chairman of the Building and Improvement Committee lost his seat and was replaced by a councillor sympathetic to the builders. In 1866 Bradford Council caved in and revised the bylaw to permit construction of back-to-backs 'provided they met stringent requirements for space, ventilation, water supply and sanitary provision'. These 'tunnel backs', as they became known, became Bradford's major form of working-class housing during the next twenty years. Profit was obviously the determining factor. No back-to-backs were approved after the 1870 bylaw but the builders had enough approvals in hand to allow them to go on building them into the 1890s.

Ripley was far from convinced and questioned the motives of the construction companies. In November 1865, frustrated by the vested interests of builders in relation to construction of affordable housing and the dithering of the council, Ripley issued a prospectus for the construction of 300 'Working-men's dwellings' on his own land: four-bedroom through houses with rear yards and front gardens and an internal WC. These houses were to be sold to small landlords and owner-occupiers. Lighting, ventilation, heating, storage, privacy and open space were taken into consideration and the design of the Ripley Ville houses incorporated these enhanced standards, and in a number of ways exceeded them.

By the time Ripley Ville was established there was a long tradition of industry-based model villages in England, all with their own variations. They included Robert Owen's and David Dale's 1786 New Lanark; Swindon Railway Village (1840s); Titus Salt's Saltaire (1853); Edward Akroyd's Akroydon, near Halifax (1859); Nenthead, Cumberland (1861); and New Sharlston Colliery Village, near Wakefield (1864). Ripley was followed by, among many others all with significant variations, Cadbury's Bournville; James Reckitt's Quaker garden village in Hull in 1908; Joseph Rowntree's New Earswick, near York (1902); and Lever's Port Sunlight.

One thing that the visionary and enlightened industrialists behind these settlements had in common was the firm belief that a contented, comfortable and well-nourished workforce was a productive workforce. Living in overcrowded, insanitary and damp slums with family life lubricated with drink and punctuated with domestic violence and regular visits to the pawnbroker was not conducive to achieving targets or meeting orders. While profit margins were never compromised – they always came first – Henry Ripley, Cadbury, Rowntree and others all saw that margins were more achievable, market share was more winnable and competition was more beatable if the men and women on the shop floor or on the road were in a fit state to put in a productive day's work.

On 24 January 1866 planning permission to build 254 houses was granted. Invitations to tender went out for 200 houses plus one school, approval for which was given 8 June 1867. All the houses were built by early 1868. Thirteen terraces of houses along four residential

Cadbury's Bournville.

Lever's Port Sunlight.

Rowntree's New Earswick, near York.

Reckitt's garden village in Hull.

streets were laid out on a north–south axis. Early builds were completed with inside toilets in the cellar – later retro-fitted with external ash closets – while later versions had outside external ash closets from the start. WCs were the preserve of the middle classes, virtually unknown in working-class houses – except for those originally planned in Ripley Ville.

By 1871 the site was bounded by railway lines on three sides, on a triangle of land between east and west Bowling and to the north of Bowling Dye Works. (Bowling) Hall Lane lay to the east.

In December 1868 the Bradford Ten Churches Building Committee agreed to build a church in Ripley Ville on land donated by Ripley – St Bartholomew's Church was consecrated in December 1872. Ten almshouses were built by Ripley in 1881.

So rose Ripley Ville, a townscape which remained intact for 100 or so years. The development featured 196 houses with three sizes. Type 1 houses had two large ground-floor rooms and a scullery in a back extension. The cellar was fitted out as a 'cellar kitchen' with a sink and range. The cellar also contained a WC and a coal store. Type 2 houses boasted a large front ground-floor room and a smaller back room. The basement contained a storage cellar, WC in houses built under tenders 1 and 2 and coal store. Type 3 houses had a single 'through room' and small scullery on the ground floor. The basement contained a storage cellar, a coal store and a second enclosure. No WCs were fitted to Type 3 houses. All lived-in rooms had gas lighting and a fireplace or range. Fireplaces in the bedrooms were decorative cast iron.

As in many other model villages, selling alcohol was prohibited although the 1872 Smith's Directory lists Stephen Gibson of No. 2 Linton Street as a grocer, tea dealer and beer retailer.

Outside a Ripley terrace: Vere Street, 1958.

Ripley houses: front elevation.

There was no pub, but residents could drink at the nearby Locomotive Inn (which existed before Ripley Ville) at No. 7 Ellen Street, or in Hall Lane at the Bowling Hotel. Four other beer retailers are recorded in Smith's Directory. An inn called the Gibson Arms on Linton Street and part of the village seems to have been converted from two properties at some point.

Employment by Ripley was never a qualification for Ripley Ville residency. When (from 1881) Sir Henry Ripley died in 1882, his younger son, also Henry, took over as manager of the dye works. Ownership and control of the dye works passed, in 1899, to the Bradford Dyers Association, marking the end of the Ripley family association with the works or with Ripley Ville.

Ripleyville Houses – Treatments of Rear Elevations Drawn Jan 2013

Type 1 Houses		Type 2 Houses	Type 3 House
Right handed "up" house	Left handed "up" house	Right handed "down " houses	Right handed "up" house
18 Vere Street	20 Vere Street	3 Ripley Terrace 1 Ripley Terrace	8 Saville Street

Ripley houses: rear elevation.

MOORSIDE MILLS: BRADFORD INDUSTRIAL MUSEUM

Moorside Mill opened in 1875 and grew into a medium-sized factory, employing around 100 workers, focusing on worsted yarn for weaving. Originally powered by steam engines, Moorside Mills was converted to electricity in the early twentieth century. The business grew significantly during the First World War when worsted was needed in prodigious quantities for military uniforms. The mill's working life ended in 1970; Bradford Corporation bought Moorside Mill and housed an industrial museum there to preserve Bradford's industrial heritage.

Moorside Mill, now Bradford Industrial Museum. (Photograph by Linda Spashett)

Machines in the motive power room with a power-relay system on the ceiling. (Photograph by Linda Spashett)

Typesetting equipment and printing presses in printing gallery. (Photograph by Linda Spashett)

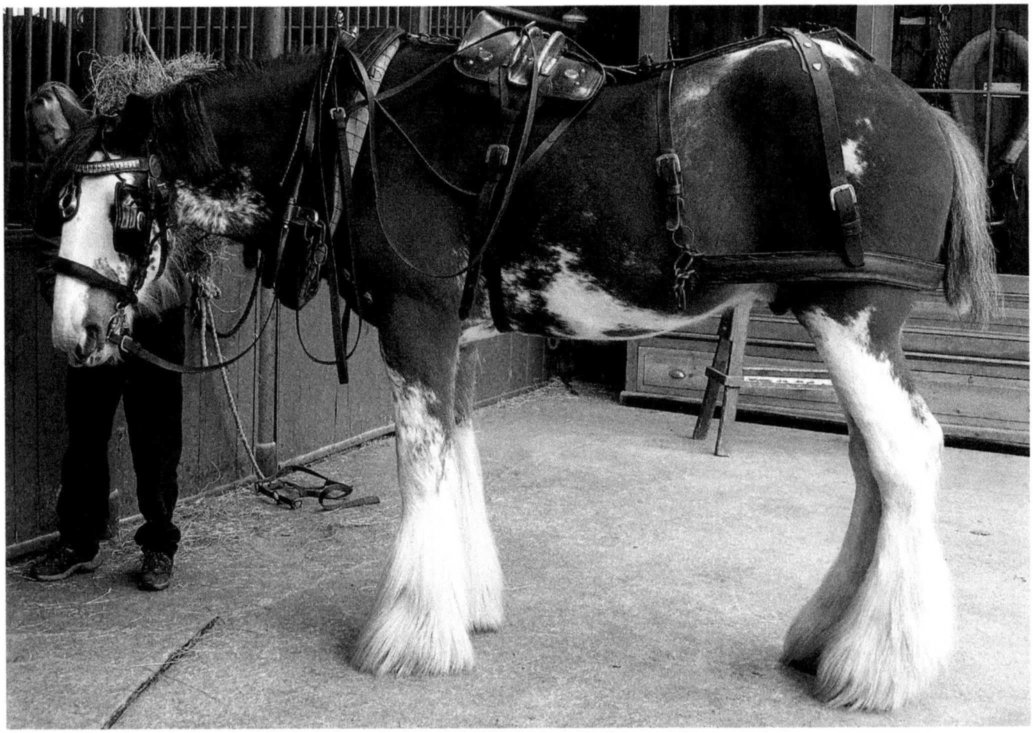

A dray horse being harnessed at Bradford Industrial Museum. (Photograph by Linda Spashett)

Bradford Industrial Exhibition, 1904.

SALTAIRE

Titus Salt, son of Daniel Salt, a dry-salter, served a two-year apprenticeship from 1822 at the nearby worsted spinning mill of William Rouse & Sons. Salt was born in Morley. After education at Batley Grammar School he started work as an apprentice wool-stapler in Wakefield, moving on to William Rouse & Son in 1822 and then in 1824 joining his father as wool buyer and partner in Daniel Salt & Son, wool-staplers in Bradford's Piccadilly. He took over the business in 1833 when his father retired and by 1853, as a worsted stuff manufacturer using the somewhat intractable Donskoi wool from southern Russia, he became the largest employer in Bradford; his factory workers were augmented by numerous outworkers combing and weaving in their homes in Little Horton, Baildon and Allerton. Always innovative, in 1836 he started using alpaca wool known as Orleans Cloth, much sought after for modish ladies' dresses; in 1837 he was using cotton warps. Charles Dickens describes how Salt came upon alpaca at C. W. & F. Foozle & Co. in a story in his magazine, *Household Words*. Queen Victoria, no less, sent him the wool from her two alpacas to make into cloth for her dresses. By 1845 Salt had made his fortune.

Before Saltaire, Titus Salt lived an active public life. A champion of radical causes, he fought the domination of the Anglican Church and church rates, supported the Anti-Corn League and Society and was an alderman. He was at the forefront of the campaign to win Bradford's incorporation in 1847; incorporation was a contentious issue with professionals, ratepayers and industrialists split down the middle. Salt was the town's second mayor, from 1848–49, and later Deputy Lieutenant for the West Riding of Yorkshire. He commissioned a report on the moral conditions in the town, which led to the foundation of the Bradford Town Mission, Peel Park (the city's first park) and the Female Educational Institute. The year 1857 saw him take on the presidency of the Bradford Chamber of Commerce; he was Liberal Member of Parliament for Bradford from 1859 until 1861. In 1869 he was created a Baronet by Queen Victoria; Napoleon III made him a Knight of the Legion of Honour. Salt died in 1876 and is buried at Saltaire Congregational Church. A reputed 100,000 mourners lined the funeral route.

During Salt's time, as we have seen, Bradford was one of the most polluted towns in England. Sewage routinely flowed undiluted into Bradford Canal (the 'River Stink') and Bradford Beck – the principal source of drinking water from the river, causing outbreaks of cholera and typhoid. Incredibly, some defended the canal – we can see how they may have been blind to the squalor that flowed past them, but it is hard to understand how they failed to register

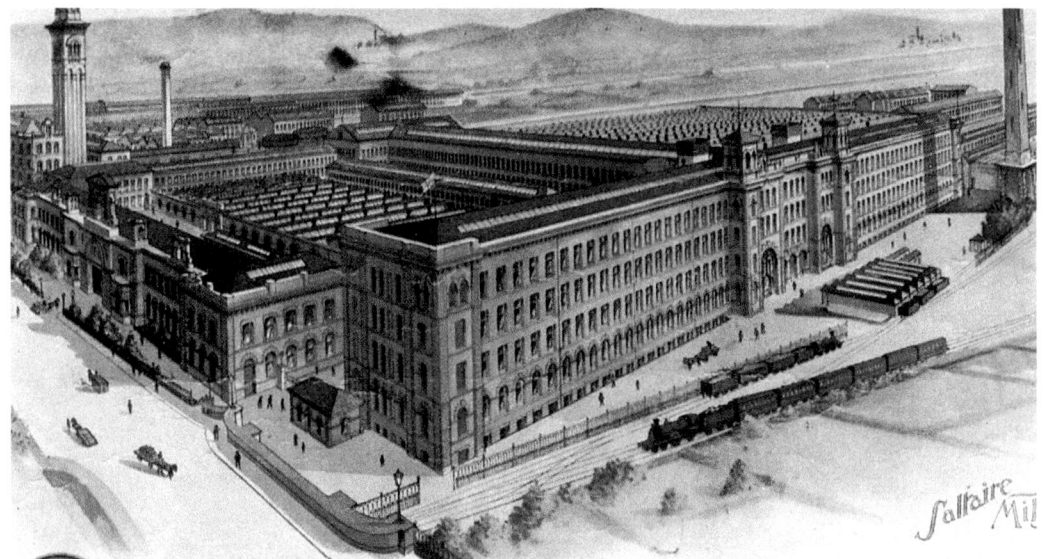

SALTAIRE

Above: The impressive campanile is one of the most aesthetic industrial chimneys ever built. It is based on the campanile on the Basilica Santa Maria Gloriosa in dei Frari in Venice. That campanile, the second tallest in the city after San Marco's, was completed in 1396. Titian is buried in the Frari. Salt's campanile was a worthy effort to maintain the character and pleasant atmosphere of Victoria Road.

Left: Salt's Mill in Saltaire from above showing the close relationship between mill and workers' housing. It was taken by C. H. Wood and is entitled *The Mill, an Aeriel View – the Finest Mill in Europe.*

the overpowering smell. Just as incredulously, some, notably a councillor called Baxendale, described the choking smoke billowing around the town as 'a good thing'. The satirists had a field day:

How beautiful is the smoke
The Bradford smoke;
Pouring from numberless chimney stacks,
Condensing and falling in showers of 'blacks'.
All around
Upon the ground
In lane and yard and street…
How beautiful is the smoke?

A mere 30 per cent of children born to wool combers lived to see the age of fifteen. In the fifty years between 1801 and 1851, fuelled by the explosion in the local worsted cloth industry and its relentless mechanisation and the concomitant dye works, the population of Bradford also exploded from 16,000 to 104,000, creating a massive overcrowding problem and all its associated issues.

Georg Weerth, the radical German pamphleteer writer friend of Marx and Engels, in between researching the impact of the Industrial Revolution on the relationship between property owner and the workers, worked in Bradford as a representative for a textile firm. In 1846 he described the town in *Neue Rheinische Zeitung* as follows:

Every other factory town in England is a paradise in comparison to this hole. In Manchester the air lies like lead upon you; in Birmingham it is just as if you were sitting with your nose in a stove pipe; in Leeds you have to cough with the dust and the stink as if you had swallowed a pound of Cayenne pepper in one go – but you can put up with all that. In Bradford, however, you think you have been lodged with the devil incarnate. If anyone wants to feel how a poor sinner is tormented in Purgatory, let him travel to Bradford.

Canal basin in Bradford around 1840 – the end of the Bradford Canal. The canal was a seething reservoir of filth and disease exuding the stench and gases of excrement and rotting rubbish.

Salt Mills from the canal today – somewhat cleaner.

Tired of Bradford's smoke and pollution and mindful of the health hazards it fostered, Salt tried to improve the environment in 1842 by introducing a device called the Rodda Smoke Burner into all his factories. This gave off comparatively little pollution. His attempts to get others to use it were unsuccessful. The year 1849 saw Titus Salt taking 3,000 workers on a railway excursion to Malham and Gordale Scar in the nearby Yorkshire Dales, where all concerned got a glimpse of a very different world. In 1850, galvanised by the prospect of this other world and by the cholera outbreak the previous year, and frustrated by the selfish anathema of his fellow factory owners, he decided he would build not just a mill large enough to consolidate his existing five mills on one site, but also a village for his workers to live in. But not in Bradford.

Salt bought Dixon's Mill estate 4 miles from the centre of Bradford. This semi-pastoral setting had the commercial advantages of being on the River Aire, on the Leeds–Skipton Railway, on Bramley Turnpike and the Leeds–Liverpool Canal. The nearby New York Delf Quarry provided much of the stone needed for the new mill and the village.

> The site chosen for Saltaire is, in many ways, desirable. The scenery in the immediate neighbourhood is romantic, rural and beautiful. A better-looking body of factory 'hands' than those in Saltaire I have not seen. They are far above the average of their class in Lancashire, and are considerably above the majority in Yorkshire.
>
> Sam Kydd, *The Reynolds*, 29 November 1857.

At six storeys high and 180 yards long, and with a floor space of over 11 acres, the ergonomic mill was the biggest and most modern in Europe. Output exceeded 30,000 yards of cloth per day, the weaving shed housed an incredible 1,200 power looms.

Poverty in Bradford, soon to be a thing of the past for Salt's workers.

Buckden in Wharfedale, not far from Malham and a world apart from Bradford.

The aim of the alpaca spinning process here was to produce alpaca worsted – a mixed cloth consisting of cotton or silk warp threads and wool weft threads. Salt's particular gift was in perfecting machinery that would spin difficult fibres, such as long and fine Donskoi wool. However, his crowning achievement was in establishing how to spin alpaca and mohair from angora goats. This resulted in 'lustre cloth', called that because it looked and felt like silk but cost a mere fraction of it. The process started with wool sorting, when imports from South America and Australia were expertly graded and sorted by quality. Impurities were then removed and forced into basins filled with soap, water and alkali. Once dried it was carded and combed through a Noble carding machine, which separated the long from the short fibres. Now it was ready for drawing and cap, flyer and ring spinning.

This engraving shows workers milling around Victoria Road in 1865, getting off the Bradford train and heading to work at the factory. The Victoria Hall and the Sunday school are visible in the background.

But alpaca was not without its problems. Roger Clarke explains:
It was possible to produce alpaca cloth without dyeing, using the natural colours of the fibre (which is hair, not wool). It ranges from black to white with 24 colours in between including four shades of grey, creams, beiges, browns etc. However, the sorting of these colours into large enough batches to satisfy the growing textile industry was impractical. Economies of scale could not be achieved, and so dyeing was the only solution. But Titus was producing worsted cloth, a mixed cloth with a cotton warp and an alpaca or wool weft. The combination of a vegetable with an animal fibres presented problems for the dyer; and indeed when wool and cotton were first combined it was the practice to dye them separately, since cotton was not as amenable to permanent dyes as wool. The techniques of dyeing them together were mastered by Edward Ripley and Son of Bowling in Bradford in 1837 and generously shared within the industry. When Titus opened his Saltaire Mill in 1853, the industry was still using natural dyes but with improved mordants.

In 1868, Titus built New Mill on the north side of the Leeds/Liverpool canal, and used it to house a new dye works. Significant changes had been made in the dyeing process with the introduction of aniline dyes.

Noise and industrial injuries were reduced by locating much of the machinery underground. Large flues removed smoke, dust and dirt from the atmosphere and from the factory floor. Fire safety equipment was state of the art. The heavily subsidised canteen was supplemented with facilities for workers to bring in their own food and cook on site.

A 1902 image of the spinning department. The paraphernalia on the ceiling are decorations for the coronation of Edward VII, which was delayed while he recovered from peritonitis.

With something like the precision of a military operation, this is ring-twisting in action in the mid-1920s. The women are working dolly-roller ring-twisting machines, which twist single yarns together and turn out strong, multi-layer yarns. A winding machine then sends them on to bobbins or pirns, which fit onto the shuttle carrying the weft (the horizontal thread) between the warp (vertical thread) during the weaving process on the loom.

Two fourteen-year-old winders at the mill in 1930, namely Lilian Marsden and her friend Phyllis. Lilian is carrying a hook on the string round her waist, which was used to wind the yarn onto the spinning frame.

The weaving department around the end of the Second World War. The woman here is fixing a pirn of weft into a boat-shaped shuttle.

Knocking-off time at the mill.

Simon Palmer's striking watercolour of Titus Salt surveying his Saltaire in an *Alice in Wonderland*-type scene, complete with huge timepiece and adoring residents.

A Simon Palmer watercolour, which neatly captures Salt's dislike of the public display of washing, showing a remorseful housewife after being rebuked by Salt.

Titus Salt was evidently influenced by Disraeli's novels *Coningsby* and particularly by Mr Trafford in *Sybil*. The driving force, though, was surely a desire to achieve efficiencies on the shop floor with efficient plant and a contented workforce – in short to maximise profits while satisfying a desire to improve the social and industrial welfare of his workers, concepts which many of his contemporaries thought mutually exclusive.

Up to 2,500 employees were ferried from Bradford to Saltaire on chartered trains each working day. To eliminate this tiring and tiresome commute, to maximise the output and efficiency of his workforce, and in line with his belief in the 'morale economy of manufactures', Salt set about building the village of Saltaire for his 3,500 workers. Between 1852 and 1872 he constructed 850 houses, complementing these with social and recreational facilities: a park, church, schools, hospital (originally a casualty ward for mill accidents but later a cottage hospital), library and shops. There was, however, neither a public house nor pawnshop.

As in other industrial villages, the new houses were far superior to the stock that the workers were used to. Clean, fresh water was piped into each house from Saltaire's own 500,000-gallon reservoir. Gas provided lighting and heating and each home had its own (outside) toilet. Salt also provided public baths and wash houses in Amelia Street to encourage public hygiene. During the cholera epidemic he distributed disinfectant to the residents.

The houses in Saltaire covered 25 acres; the population in 1871 was 4,389. The type of house you received corresponded to where you stood in the social hierarchy. Workers had two bedrooms, a living room, cellar pantry and a kitchen – all basically decorated. Overlookers had three bedrooms, a sitting room, scullery kitchen, cellar and a small front garden – decorated

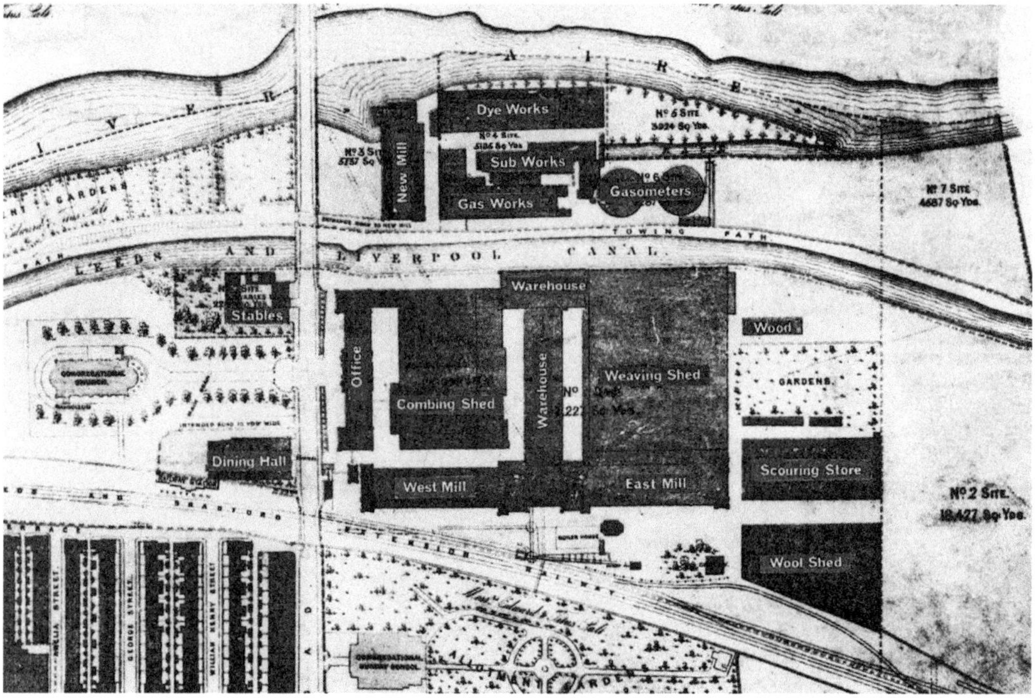

The Saltaire factory complex in 1884.

A typical Saltaire terrace.

in early Renaissance style. There were three-storey houses in Albert and Caroline Streets intended as lodging houses. The baths and wash houses were at the top of Amelia Street.

Of course, a town and workforce the size of Saltaire brought with it the need for ancillary services and businesses. The images on pages 57 and 58 show the local school and teacher, steam tram crew, and the fire service.

Saltaire consisted of twenty-nine streets and 850 stone-built houses. (Photograph: Salt Estates)

A witty allusion from 2016 to Titus Salt's temperance in Saltaire.

Practical arithmetic on 23 July 1925 at the Albert Road Mixed School. The effects of smoking on health were largely unknown in those days and may justify the appearance of the advertisement for 'Will's Gold Flake' at the front of the class.

Some cross-looking steam tram crewmen – obviously not sharing the joke with the conductor. Steam trams were introduced in 1883.

The Saltaire Fire Brigade outside the mill in 1935. Volunteers provided firewatching cover for the mill and the village.

SHIPLEY

Shipley lies next door to Saltaire, some 3.5 miles north of Bradford centre, and like Saltaire is almost a suburb. Shipley had a long reputation for sheep grazing, so wool was in good supply, and the Aire was a ready source of water for powering watermills and cleaning processes. By 1559 there were three fulling mills in Shipley: Hirst Mill, Dixon Mill and New Hirst Mill. Hirst Mill dates back to the thirteenth century. Dixon Mill and New Hirst Mill were built in 1635 and 1745 respectively, and by the late eighteenth century between 9,000 and 10,000 pieces of broadcloth were being fulled annually at Shipley's mills. Much of the work was done in workers' cottages, which had 'loomshops' for spinning yarn. Examples of home workshops can be seen in the cottages at Jane Hills along the canal in Saltaire.

Industrialisation put an end to the cottage industry. Providence Mill, Ashley Mill, Prospect Mill, Red Beck Mill on Heaton Beck (c. 1815), Well Croft Mill (c. 1840s) and Whiting Mill on Briggate all took over production. These smaller mills ceded to larger concerns, which could combine all the processes of worsted production on one site. The first was Joseph Hargreaves' Airedale Mills (demolished in the 1970s), Salts Mill, Well Croft Mill (demolished – 1950s) and Victoria Mills near the canal. By 1876 the big four worsted firms in Shipley – namely, Hargreaves, Salt's, Mason's and Denby's – were employing 6,900 workers in total. The following list, though far from complete, gives a picture of the activity in and around Shipley:

- Gill Mill in Tong Park, Baildon (1778), had been spinning worsted since 1790, and was enlarged by William Denby & Sons in 1853.
- Providence Mill, Shipley, was a small woollen mill built in 1796, later converted to worsted spinning.
- Red Beck Mill, Shipley Fields, Shipley (1815), was the first mill in Shipley to be built for worsted.
- Old Whiting Mill, Shipley. In 1822 James Warbrick, a Bradford worsted spinner, had a power loom built there. One day a mob of local weavers destroyed the loom, parading the wreckage through the streets.
- Union Mill, Low Well, Shipley. Built in 1823, with a 40-hp steam engine, by Wilcox, Bradley & Co. In 1833 it was employing eighty-three hands in scribbling and fulling for the domestic woollen trade.
- Wellcroft Mill in the centre of Shipley (1845) was built by William Denby Jr, and later enlarged.

- Airedale Mills, Baildon Bridge, Shipley, was a large factory built in 1850 by Joseph Hargreaves.
- Sir Titus Salt's Mill, Saltaire (1853).
- Henry Mason's Victoria Mill, Shipley (1875).

Three generations of the Wright family owned Hirst Mill. Joseph Wright's *Dialect Dictionary* gives us the following interesting definitions:

FAN: sheets of sacking on a rotating wooden frame, causing a wind used in winnowing corn, i.e. blowing away the chaff from the grain. This one is probably water driven.
PICK: a tool used to dress a millstone and prepare it for grinding.
STROAKE, PECK: almost certainly measuring vessels. A stroke is two pecks; four pecks make a bushel (8 gallons). A stroke is also a smooth straight piece of wood with which the surplus grain is struck off to level it with the rim of the measure.
MULCTURE: a certain fraction of the meal taken as payment in kind by the miller.
ARK: a meal chest.
KILN: for drying the grain before grinding. A kiln hair is possibly a screen woven of hair for use in the drying process.
KITT: a wooden vessel.
GRINDLESTONE: a grindstone
SWAPE: the handle of a grindstone, which sweeps out a circle when in use.
GAVELOCK: an iron crowbar or lever.
POYTE/POTE: meaning poker.
MAULE: a hammer.
NADGE: an adze, a carpenter's hand tool.

Boots, nails and bricks were also made in Shipley, while the twenty or so quarries in the vicinity made quarrying and building another significant local industry. W. Fletcher & Son,

Shipley quickly became everything that Saltaire was not – another polluted Bradford.

dry-salter and manufacturing chemist, were located at the Dale Street works. Fletcher's were famous for cooking salt – pure and 'untouched by hand' – pumice stone, baking powder, 'Sunshine' furniture cream, soup tablets and 'Country Relish'. They had significant export markets in South Africa and Canada. The horse-drawn transport fleet was housed in stables that could accommodate seventeen horses.

C. F. Taylor's Airedale Mill pictured on the left in the Otley Road.

A factory shop at Fletcher's? Tubs of Colman's starch in good supply.

W. Fletcher & Son.

Airedale Mills was where the Denby Brothers built and operated Providence Mill, one of the UK's first steam-driven mills, in 1796. It was used for cloth scribbling. The mill was rebuilt in 1861 after a boiler explosion in 1811.

The scribbler worked in the clothiers workshop, oiling the wool to make it easier to work with. Olive oil, known as Gallipoli oil, was imported through Bristol from Mediterranean countries. After 1675, scribblers used hand cards to draw the wool over a scribbling horse – a frame covered with iron teeth set in leather leaves. Scribbling work was often given to older or disabled workers. From the 1790s, scribbling engines took over this work. These machines were originally horse powered but were later worked by water power and then steam. The scribbler is now the name of the first part of a carding set, a modern carding machine.

As with other growing industrial towns, though, Shipley quickly became everything that Saltaire was not: dreadfully overcrowded, polluted, insanitary and a reservoir for deadly diseases such as cholera, scarlet fever, smallpox and malnutrition.

FORGOTTEN COTTON

'Cotton in Lancashire; wool in Yorkshire' – or so the old adage goes. But there was an interpolator in Yorkshire: cotton. After 1835 it is quite true that wool was the Yorkshire textile of choice, but before that cotton mills were much in evidence; their spinning machines later switched from cotton to wool. Towns like Keighley and Todmorden owe their expansion to cotton. Bradford too had its share of cotton mills. This apparent intrusion comes as less of a surprise when we consider that more than 40 per cent of the country's cotton workers in the late eighteenth and nineteenth centuries were employed outside of Lancashire – the county with the supposed monopoly on the industry – in fifteen other counties of England and Wales.

Moreover, there was significant cooperation and interaction between the Yorkshire cotton and Yorkshire wool business, which included shared capital, entrepreneurship, movements of labour and the supply of cotton to wool textile manufacture.

Cotton plant, Ware County, Georgia, 2015. (Photograph by Bubba73 [Jud McCranie])

Above: The Lancashire cotton famine (1861–65) was a serious depression in the cotton industry stimulated by overproduction in a time of contracting world markets.

Left: Some of the wonderful cotton industry paraphernalia on display in the Bird in Hand pub in Stockport.

Ironically, Yorkshire has Lancashire to thank for the growth in cotton manufacture it experienced at the end of the eighteenth century. Yorkshire cotton mills had been built to stave off yarn shortages among Lancashire handloom weavers. Between 1795 and 1815 the increasing yarn output in the growing number of Yorkshire cotton mills led to an increase in cotton manufacture. This was facilitated and expedited by the fact that it was relatively easy to switch from handloom weaving worsted cloth – already well established, of course – to cotton cloth for which demand was increasing and which was well paid. Furthermore, it was not difficult to convert mills to cotton spinning and workers at home could work to their own hours and for a number of different masters depending on rates of pay offered, moving back to weaving worsted cloth according to market demand.

A scene inside the Quarry Mill Museum, Styal – a former cotton mill.

A cotton-weaving workshop at Armley Mills, Leeds Industrial Museum, in 2016.

Redundant cotton mills in Bingley.

One hotspot of cotton weaving was the Horton area of Bradford. Carriers were hired to take cloth to Manchester and to other centres; warps were brought back on the three-day return journey to Bradford. Cotton-spinning mills were opened by John and Benjamin Knight in 1806 in Great Horton. Other mills went up in Little Horton and Horton Green as well and the industry thrived, until, that is, the collapse of a key Manchester merchanting house sent many of them to the wall. Many then converted to worsted manufacturing, including Abraham Balme and Samuel Swaine. Another cotton-spinning mill was built at Idle and others in Bradford – Holme Mill and Rand's Mill, both of whom went over to worsted in 1810. John Knowles was the Yorkshire cotton king, whose kingdom extended not just around Bradford but around the country as a whole. He ran Hallas Bridge Mill and Bent Mill on the outskirts of Bradford. His son, John Wilkinson Knowles, took over the business but even the Knowles succumbed to the 1826 recession.

In the meantime, in 1802 William Ratcliffe of Stockport patented a dandy loom, a framed handloom that represented an intermediate stage between home or workshop weaving and factory-based power loom weaving. Higher quality cloth was assured. We find evidence of dandy loom workshops in Kettlewell, Todmorden, Addingham and Bradford. A chronic shortage of yarn meant that home workers were increasingly forced into workshops in premises converted by manufacturers who could supply the warp and weft: loss of independence had to be traded off against a weekly wage. The dandy loom weaver working in a small workshop would rent the loom for 10½d a week and in 1825 could expect to earn 5s a week.

In the mid-1830s the industry was far from consistent or unified: there were around twice as many weavers operating a variety of different handlooms as there were power looms. The dandy loom increased productivity of a handloom weaver by as much as 50 per cent.

Doncaster saw the first attempts at cotton power-loom weaving in 1786 in a short-lived enterprise by Edmund Cartwright using twenty looms. There were other cotton-spinning mills at nearby Balby (1792) and in Doncaster's Fishergate (1790). We have to wait until 1821 before the next Yorkshire foray into cotton – at William Hegginbottom's power loom weaving at Saddleworth. This was followed in 1825 and 1826 by power looms installed at Low Mill, Addingham and at Gargrave, coinciding with a marked downturn in trade. Understandably, the handloom weavers associated the power looms with plummeting prices for their finished goods; troops had to be called in to defend the looms at both locations from serious outbreaks of Luddism.

But power looms prevailed and by 1835 twenty-four West Yorkshire mills could boast cotton power looms among their assets. That same year Baines's *History of the Cotton Manufacture in Great Britain* highlighted cotton mills in the Calder, Aire and Wharfe valleys, in Saddleworth, Todmorden, Halifax, Skipton, Keighley, Addingham, Bingley and elsewhere.

In Bradford, or at least in the centre, cotton mill development was hampered by the absence of suitable water. In addition, when cotton mill owner John Buckley proposed a steam-powered cotton mill in Manchester Road in 1793 he was rejected. By 1810 things had changed and cotton weaving was well established in Bradford for a short period, particularly around Great and Little Horton and Allerton. Here are some details about some of the cotton mills in the Bradford area:

- Castlefield Mill, Bingley (1790), was bought by Peter Garforth Jr around 1800, who already had cotton mills at Skipton, Bell Busk and Sedbergh. It was still operating in 1833, employing 130 people on thirty-one spinning frames with seventy-two spindles each.
- Bent Mill, Wilsden (1799), was owned by John Knowles, as noted above, and damaged by the 1826 crisis. At its peak it had 2,312 throstle spindles and 4,248 mule spindles. Bent Mill survived into the 1830s when it was employing sixty-one workers.

- Elmtree Mill (1811) was built for worsted spinning, converted to cotton, then to cottages.
- Cullingworth Mill was used for cotton around 1830.
- Hallas Bridge Mill, Wilsden (1802), was bought by John Knowles around 1812. It was three storeys high and had twenty-four cottages.
- Goit Stock Mill, Harden, was owned by Horsfall & Co. from 1797, who had a cotton warehouse in Bridge Street, Bradford. It converted to a woolstaplers and worsted manufacturers.
- Wilsden Mills, Wilsden (c. 1792), was four storeys high and was built next to a corn mill. John Smith, one of the partners from 1803, went insane in 1816, although this was kept secret until 1822. A worsted mill was built next door. The corn mill operated eight mules with 1,200 spindles and twelve throstles with 1,200 spindles. The estate also included a counting house, five cottages and two warehouses. The mills converted to worsted after 1822, as did the Old Mill in Wilsden with its sixteen frames and forty-eight spindles.
- Idle Cotton Mill comprised two mills erected on the site of a former corn mill – one for scribbling and carding, the other for cotton. In 1803 it employed twenty-seven workers in its five storeys. In 1826 the mill converted to worsted.
- Knight's Mill, Great Horton, Bradford (1806), was four storeys high and was built by John Knight, a leading player in the Bradford cotton world. Bankruptcy came in 1827. The estate included many cottages and a five-storey warehouse. The mill converted to worsted after 1827.
- Holme Mill, Bradford (1800), was the town's first steam-powered worsted mill, built by Henry Ramsbotham. Between 1803 and 1807 the mill was used for cotton spinning to meet booming demand.
- Rand's Mill, Bradford (1803), was built for worsted and cotton.

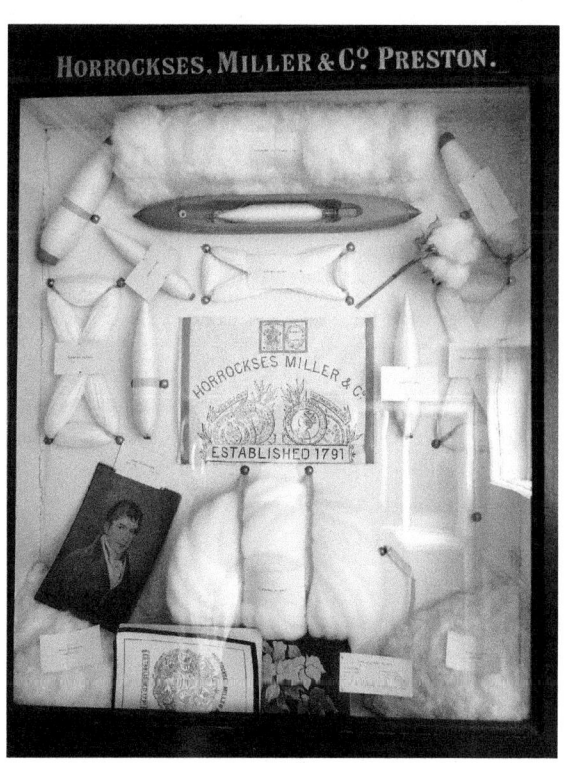

An old advertising display for a cotton manufacturer in Preston, Lancashire, showing items used in cotton textile manufacture. The items, row by row, are: finished scutcher lap, ring frame bobbin, shuttle, ring frame bobbin, weft cop, roving sliver, cotton boll, slubbing sliver, twist cop, company crest, twist cop, intermediate sliver, John Horrocks (1768 – 1804), carding sliver, raw cotton (American), book, the cotton plant, raw cotton (Egyptian). (Photograph by Richerman)

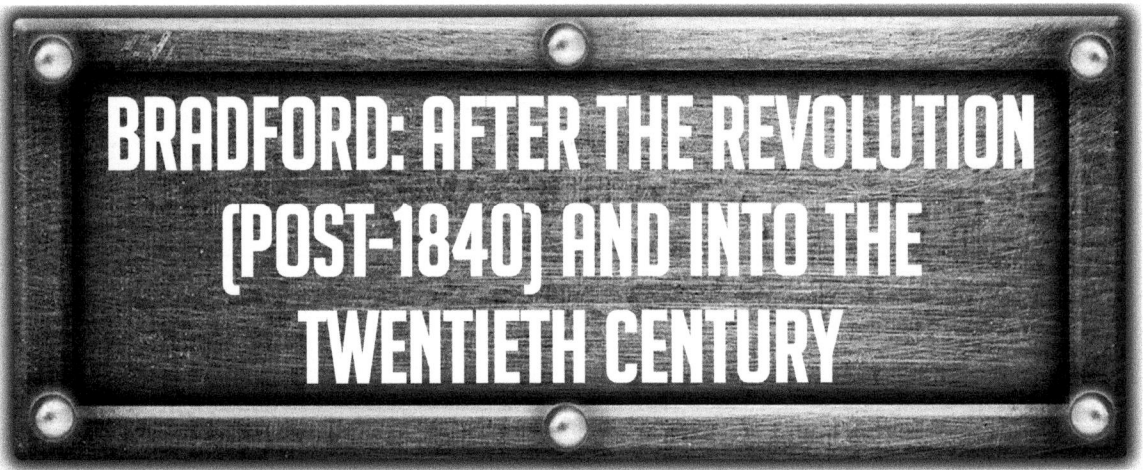

BRADFORD: AFTER THE REVOLUTION (POST-1840) AND INTO THE TWENTIETH CENTURY

IMMIGRATION

The middle of the nineteenth century saw Bradford start to emerge as a modern industrial city; indeed, Bradford was the fastest growing town in Europe. One of the catalysts for this was the large number of economic migrants who flocked to the town seeking work. Industry needs workers, and immigrants played a significant role in Bradford's emergence as a major industrial town. Bradford has been called a 'world of strangers', as at this time half its population were first-generation immigrants – from Germany, Scotland, many from Ireland and from other parts of Yorkshire and neighbouring counties. Although most of them brought rural rather than industrial occupational skill sets, they were of inestimable value to the burgeoning Bradford economy. The Irish were mainly from rural Mayo and Sligo, and by 1841 around 13 per cent of the population of Bradford had been born in Ireland, the largest number anywhere in Yorkshire. They settled in eight densely inhabited areas near the town centre, one of which was the Bedford Street area of Broomfields, which in 1861 was home to 1,162 persons of Irish descent – 19 per cent of all Irish-born persons in the borough.

During the 1820s and 1830s many of the German immigrants were Jewish merchants who went on to enjoy an active part in Bradford life. The Jewish community settled mostly in the Manningham area, numbering around 100 families, and was influential in the development of Bradford as a major exporter of woollen goods from their textile export houses, mainly located in the Little Germany district. Tsarist pogroms forced 15,000 Jews to flee Russia to Great Britain in the 1890s, and they settled mainly in East London, Leeds, Bradford and Manchester.

Charles Semon (1814–77) was a textile merchant and philanthropist from Gdansk who developed a textile export house in the town. He became the first foreign and Jewish mayor of Bradford in 1864. A philanthropist of some note, he financed and built a convalescent home in Ilkley in 1874 and transferred it to the Bradford Corporation in 1876 with an endowment for its upkeep. In his will he bequeathed £35,000 to support educational institutions in Bradford.

Jacob Behrens (1806–89) was the first foreign textile merchant to export woollen goods from Bradford. His company grew into an international multimillion-pound business. Also a philanthropist, Behrens helped set up the Bradford Chamber of Commerce in 1851. Jacob Moser (1839–1922) was also a textile merchant and a partner in the firm Edelstein, Moser & Co., which developed into another successful Bradford textile export house. Moser founded the Bradford Charity Organisation Society and the City Guild of Help.

Of the 25,000 or so Italians in Britain by 1901, half lived in London with significant numbers in Leeds, Bradford, Hull, Manchester and other cities. After the Second World War migrants came from Poland and Ukraine, and since the 1950s, to enormous local benefit to Bradford industry, from Bangladesh, India and particularly Pakistan.

RENAISSANCE

By the 1860s the major industries were well established: iron and coal, as we have seen, were both hugely important to the local economy. But, at the same time, the town was the unrivalled and unchallenged capital of the global empire of worsted textiles.

A cultural change was afoot and capitalist ideas were being challenged – in part at least. It was increasingly accepted, but by no means universally, that public good ought to prevail over private advantage. Public expenditure and business rates were necessary evils in order to provide public amenities, and to curb the excesses of industrialisation and the selfish pursuit of profit. In Bradford, to provide a town fit to be a wool world capital, the noisome Beck was culverted and a main sewer system established. A police force became an increasingly revered local institution to safeguard the establishment of a thriving local community, which included churches, chapels, friendly and improvement societies, temperance organisations, trade unions, political associations, and social and sporting clubs.

The relative beautification of the city centre accelerated from 1860 when old familiar landmarks indicative of a semi-rural past disappeared – the Manor House in Kirkgate, by now a rundown Temperance Hotel; the dilapidated Corn Mills in Aldermanbury; the Piece Hall, long-since divided into shops; and the Bowling Green Inn, redundant without its coaching traffic. Old industry, as symbolised by Cliff's Foundry, the Canal Basin and the Union Street Mill, the former headquarters of Sir Titus Salt's original alpaca empire, ceded to railways, warehouses and new thoroughfares. Financial services began to emerge with merchants and bankers setting up their offices in fine buildings in Little Germany and in the fiscal triangle of Bank Street, Kirkgate and Hustlergate. Fetid slums were swept away to make way for fine new streets – Godwin Street, Sunbridge Road and Grattan Road – on which the sun shone and where the air was more breathable. James Burnley went so far as to describe Darley Street and Godwin Street, with its new Kirkgate Market, Free Library and the Friends Provident Institution, as taking on 'a classical character' and 'par excellence, the fashionable town thoroughfare'. Market Street and the new town hall even had Burnley romantically drawing comparisons with Florence and Siena. The glorious Swan Arcade, once the old White Swan Inn, also impressed, as did the Victorian-Venetian Wool Exchange – it was 'so brand new and so imposing as to seem like a Metropolitan thoroughfare grafted on to the ancient street system'. In Bradford, in certain light, you might imagine yourself 'in some stately Continental city'. This was Bradford's heyday, and it was all built on coal, iron and ... on wool.

Industry, of one complexion or another, fostered a thriving and thrusting middle class of mill owners, upper-and middle-management bosses and executives of commerce and industry, members of the professions – doctors, solicitors, accountants, engineers, journalists and school teachers – whose numbers doubled between 1860 and 1880. They, of course, needed somewhere leafy to live. One result was that the old medieval fields of Horton and Manningham were built over to accommodate garden squares, mansions, and comfortably solid terraced houses. The new Bradford Grammar School was founded in 1871 to educate their middle-class children while the Mechanics' Institute was opened in Tyrrel Street in

Bradford University in 2017: Richmond Building, Great Horton Road, Bradford.

Bradford University in the 1960s. The university received its royal charter in 1966.

1872 to educate the increasingly literate working man, ever more curious and enquiring. The Church Institute opened on North Parade in 1873 while the Yorkshire College of Science and the Technical College developed between 1878 and 1882.

The University of Bradford's origins go back to the Mechanics' Institute, which in 1882 became the Bradford Technical College. In 1957, the Bradford Institute of Technology was formed as a College of Advanced Technology. To a large extent the university's courses and faculties reflect and promote the town's industrial heritage and provide a platform for future research and industrial development. The university inherited several engineering courses from the Bradford Institute of Technology such as Civil Engineering, still taught today. The EIMC department was founded in 1991 and developed its courses in conjunction with the School of Art, Design & Textiles at Bradford and Ilkley Community College, now known as Bradford College, and the National Museum of Photography, Film and Television, now the National Media Museum.

Local, national and world news came with *The Bradford Daily Telegraph, The Bradford Times, The Chronicle* and *Mail* and the *Bradford Observer*. The *Yorkshireman* and *The Yorkshire Magazine* elevated literacy and satisfied curiosity yet further.

SIR ISAAC HOLDEN

Sir Isaac Holden (1807–97) is remembered as the inventor of the Square Motion wool-combing machine and as a manufacturer. Having been narrowly beaten to the invention of the Lucifer match by John Walker of Stockton-on-Tees in 1827 (Walker omitted to patent his invention), in 1830 Holden moved from Glasgow to take work as a bookkeeper at Townsends' worsted factory in Cullingworth, near Bingley. From there he moved to management, devoting his time to perfecting the process of combing wool.

Sixteen years later Holden left Townsends to set up a factory making Paisley Shawl middles at Pit Lane in Bradford. This failed after two years in 1848, and he went into partnership with Samuel Lister with whom he collaborated on the Square Motion wool-combing machine, which was patented by Lister. The machine and its patent was the cause of a lifelong bitter dispute between the two men. After a successful time in France, in 1860 Holden and his sons, Angus and Edward, set up an experimental factory at Penny Oaks in Bradford and then in 1864 they opened the huge Alston Works in Thornton Road. By the 1870s Holden's factories in England and France (one at Croix near Roubaix and one at Rheims) had become the largest wool combers in the world. Together the three factories covered over 30 acres of factory floor space, employed 4,000 people, had 650 carding engines and 460 combing machines, which, before the introduction of the wool-combing machine, would have occupied 80,000 handloomers.

RIMMINGTONS

The famous Bradford chain of chemists was run by Whitworth Rimmington (b. 1873, d. 1926). His uncle, Felix Marsh Rimmington, was a respected and eminent chemist.

In 1858 Felix Marsh was called as a professional witness in a celebrated arsenic poisoning trial, uncovering the mystery of the humbug sweets poisoning. This was the accidental arsenic poisoning of more than 200 people. Twenty people died and over 200 became seriously ill when sweets inadvertently made with arsenic were sold from a market stall in Bradford. For centuries before, sugar was extremely expensive and was called 'white gold'. The government recognised the opportunities here and taxed it severely – in 1815 the tax raised from sugar in Britain was £3,000,000. To defray the costs of raw materials, sweet and chocolate manufacturers resorted to adulteration and their products were often mixed with cheaper substances, or 'daff'. 'Daff' was a concoction of harmless and not very tasty substances such as powdered limestone and plaster of Paris.

William Hardaker, known locally as 'Humbug Billy', routinely sold his sweets from a stall in the Green Market in Bradford. His supplier, James Appleton, the manufacturer of the sweets – including peppermint humbugs – used daff in his sweet production, daff that was supplied by a druggist in Shipley. Tragically, 12 lbs of arsenic trioxide were one day sold instead of the harmless daff. Both daff and arsenic trioxide are white powders and look alike; the arsenic trioxide was not properly labelled and was negligently shelved next to the daff.

The mistake went undiscovered during the manufacture of the sweets. Appleton combined 40 lbs of sugar, 12 lbs of arsenic trioxide, 4 lbs of gum, and peppermint oil to make 40 lbs of peppermint humbugs. The sweets contained enough arsenic to kill two people per humbug.

As usual, Hardaker sold the toxic humbugs from his stall. Of those who bought and ate the sweets, around twenty people died, with a further 200 or so becoming severely ill within a day or so. All involved in the production and sale were charged with manslaughter, but none were convicted.

Good did, however, come from this tragedy. There was new legislation to protect the public in the form of the 1860 Adulteration of Food and Drink Bill, which changed the way in which ingredients could be used, mixed and combined. The UK Pharmacy Act of 1868 introduced more stringent regulations regarding the handling and selling of named poisons and medicines by pharmacists. The abolition of the sugar tax in 1874 meant sugar became affordable to all, thus making daff redundant. Felix Marsh thus played a part in shaping the regulations of the Royal Pharmaceutical Society.

As Borough Analyst – Rimmington was expert in isolating and identifying chemical components – he was called to work on a suspected Jack the Ripper mutilation case in Bradford in 1888. A horse called Tommy pulled the Rimmington cart that delivered supplies and medications to different sites and patients around 1914. Rimmingtons still trades today at No. 9 Bridge Street.

Above and opposite: Four Bradford trades vans on the Canal Road: grocer's; milkman with gas fuel sack, not a mattress, removals, and chemicals = vitriol or sulphuric acid.

Three more Bradford vans and their trades: licence plates 106–198, Rook Lane, Dudley Hill; Gott's Pops, the new health sweets in Midland Road; and white goods from the Gas Department.

BUSBYS

Busbys was one of two Bradford High Street giants. This one was on Manningham Lane. It was founded by Ernest Busby on Kirkgate in 1908 with forty staff, but by the 1950s the store was keeping 830 staff in work.

Busbys closed their Kirkgate store on Easter Sunday 1930 to make the big move to Manningham Lane. The building exuded Victorian Gothic, and the logo – four marching and helmeted Coldstream Guards – became a badge of Bradford itself. The popular bargain basement rubbed shoulders with the showrooms full of luxury gowns and dresses ... and furs. Ernest Busby was himself a furrier and bought in skins from Leipzig even before the First World War. One mink coat sold for £4,600. Debenhams bought the business in August 1958, and the store closed in 1978.

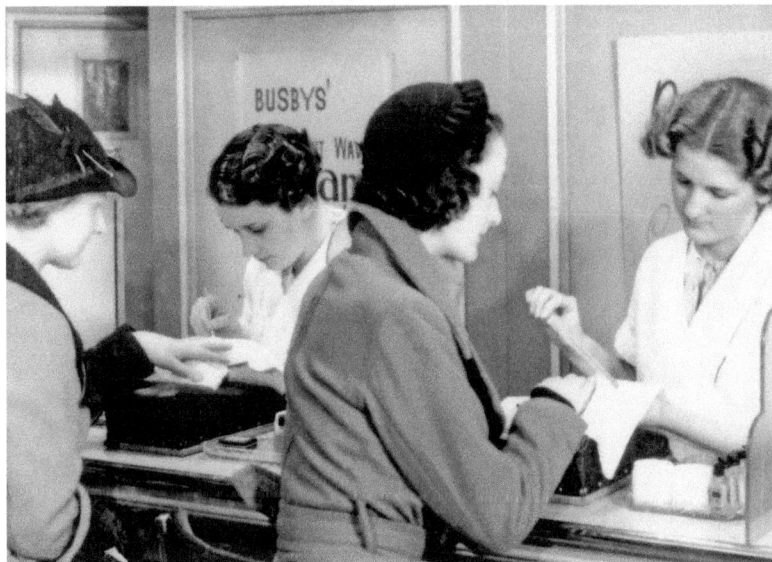

Busby nail bar in the early 1960s – and everyone thinks they are a new thing.

A part from Busbys being hauled along Drewton Street.

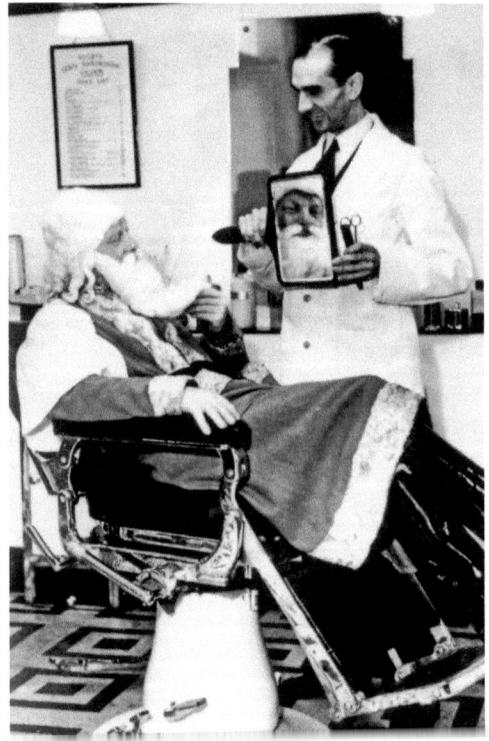

Left: Santa having a trim at Busbys.

Opposite above: Busbys.

Opposite below: A demonstration of kitchen appliances at Busbys.

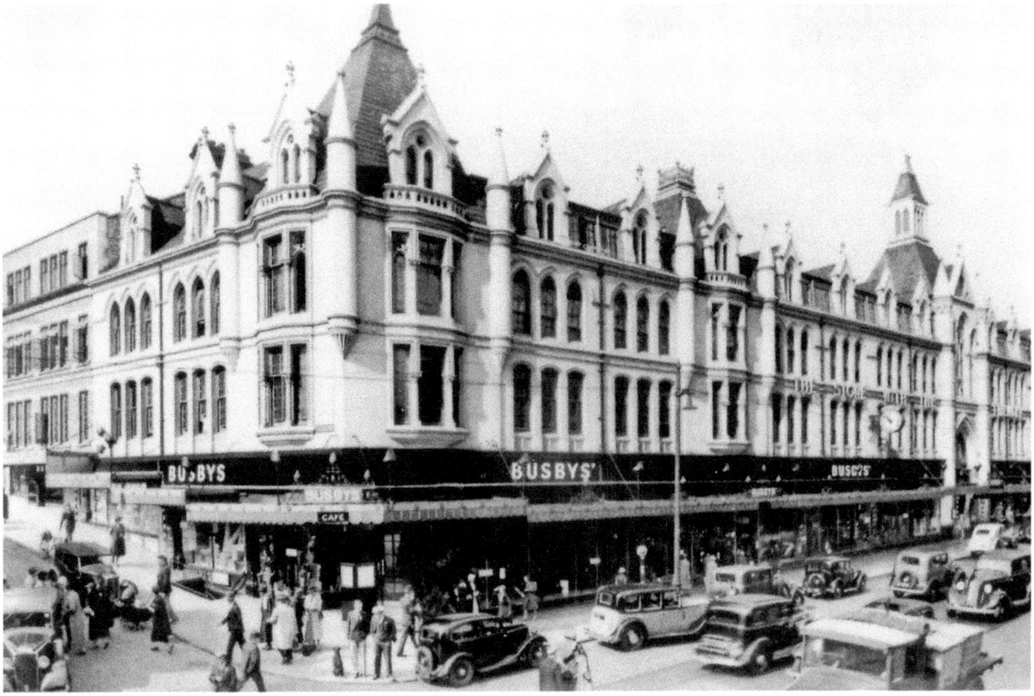
BUSBYS
BUSBYS'
CAFE

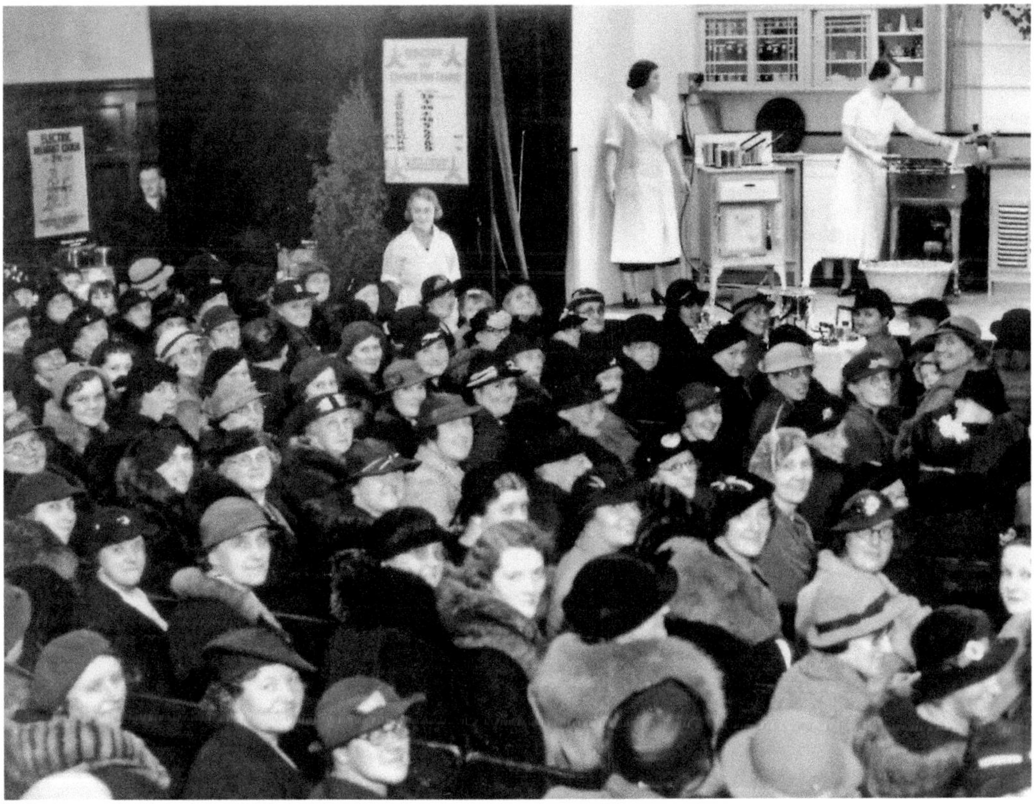

BROWN AND MUFFS

Another Bradford High Street legend. It all started in 1814 when Elizabeth Brown, a thirty-seven-year-old widow used her husband's legacy to open a drapers store at No. 11 Market Street. By 1822, the shop also boasted a bookshop and public library. In 1828 Mrs Brown went in to partnership with her son, Henry, renaming the store Brown & Son. In 1834, Elizabeth retired and left the shop to Henry. He joined up with his brother-in-law, Thomas Muff, and so Brown and Muffs arrived.

Above: Brown and Muffs.

Below: Bradford shopping in the 1960s.

The store was at the heart of a major shopping area in the town. The Venetian Gothic Wool Exchange opened in 1867 and the Italianate Swan Arcade in 1880. In 1856 there were eight or so businesses in the area including three public houses, six hairdressers and numerous grocers, jewellers and solicitors.

The year 1870 saw the original Muff building demolished to make way for the building we see today. A beauty parlour opened in 1927. In 1977 RackhamsHouse of Fraser bought the business. It closed in 1995.

Right: The Wool Exchange on Market Street.

Below: One of Bradford's older shops: Judy Barrett's in Westgate.

KIRKGATE MARKET

This impressive 1878 building replaced an earlier market. The cast-iron frame contained two 60-foot-high domes, and hugely symbolic figures of Pomona and Flora stood over the arched entrance. It was demolished in 1973. Pomona was a Roman goddess of orchard fruit and abundance. Flora was a Sabine fertility goddess of flowers and of spring.

Kirkgate Market Hall.

Pomona by Nicholas Fouché (1653–1733), now in the Szépművészeti Múzeum, Budapest.

Right: *Flora* in the Naples National Archaeological Museum, Provenance: room W26, Villa di Arianna, Stabiae.

Below: Kirkgate Market gates.

Kirkgate Market gates.

WETHERDAIR

'Wet weather Wetherdair' was one of the slogans used by this Bradford-based raincoat manufacturer. Another was, 'For Wetherdair's perfect shoulders, for Wetherdair's easy drape, for all Wetherdair's advantages – you must have a – Wetherdair - the impeccable weather coat'.

Working the doubling frame at the Wetherdair factory, 1940. (Photograph by G. H Wood)

THE JOWETT MOTOR COMPANY

The Jowett Motor Company was a prestigious motor car company operating from Bradford from 1901 to 1954, thus spanning the golden age of British motor car production. The company was founded in 1901 by brothers Benjamin (1877–1963) and William (1880–1965) Jowett, together with Arthur V. Lamb.

In the very early days the company focused on transport of the two-wheeled variety, taking advantage of the contemporary craze for bicycles and cycling. V-twin engines for driving machinery followed and some of these early engines found their way in the Bradford area into other makes of cars as replacement parts. In 1904 the name changed to the Jowett Motor Manufacturing Company based in Back Burlington Street. The first Jowett light car prototype came off the production line in February 1906; however, as the workshop was already busied with general engineering work, experiments with different engine configurations, and manufacturing the first six Scott motorbikes, the inaugural model did not go into production until 1910, after more than 25,000 miles of exhaustive trials.

The mission was to offer a low-weight vehicle at a modest price and with low running costs – in effect the United Kingdom's first real light car. The robust engine and gearbox emphasized this lightness, made largely of aluminium. The local terrain with its hills and moorland roads determined and informed the design and specification: the car's low-speed torque and gear ratios were made compatible to driving on these poor roads, where top speeds and speedy acceleration were of secondary importance.

Idle workers on the Javelin assembly line at Jowett Cars Ltd in Idle, near Bradford. The Jowett Javelin was an executive car produced from 1947 to 1953. A 1953 model boasted a top speed of 82.4 mph (132.6 km/h) accelerating from 0–60 mph (97 km/h) In 20.9 seconds. Fuel consumption was 29.1 miles per gallon. The car cost £1,207 including taxes.

Jowett's from the air.

In the First World War the factory was converted to munitions manufacture. After the armistice in 1919, a new site was bought at Springfield Works, Bradford Road, Idle, on the site of a disused quarry. The first vehicle to come out of here was the Jowett Seven using an enlarged version of the pre-war flat twin. Commercial vehicles based on the car chassis were manufactured from 1922 and became an increasingly important part of the company's portfolio and output. A fire briefly interrupted production in September 1931.

The Flying Fox took off in 1933 and Jowett Kestrel was launched in 1934 with a four-speed gearbox. In 1935 the Jowett Weasel sports tourer arrived. The Second World War halted car production in 1940 but engine production for motor-generator sets continued apace alongside aircraft components and other materiel. The engine was used as a generator set and in the Jowett engine-powered fire pump. Jowett's was bought by property developer Charles Clore in 1945, who sold it in 1947 to Lazard Brothers.

The commercial side of the business now included a light lorry, the Bradford van, two versions of an estate car called the Utility, and the popular streamlined Jowett Javelin. Over 70,000 were made over seven years. In 1950 this was joined by the Jowett Jupiter Javelin sports car. In 1952 the bottom fell out of the export market. Sales fell by 75 per cent in 1952 on top of unexciting, sluggish domestic sales. Jupiters were still popular and were built up to the end of 1954.

Jowett's sold their factory to International Harvester, tractor builders at the site until the early 1980s. The factory was demolished in 1983. Jowett converted to manufacturing aircraft parts for the Blackburn & General Aircraft Company in a former woollen mill at Howden Clough, Birstall, near Batley. Jowett was taken over by Blackburn in 1956.

Jowett 10 four-cylinder, 1937.

Jowett 8 – pre-First World War.

A 7-hp Blackbird, 1932.

Jowett Jupiter, two-seater sports car.

Jowett Morrison's van: 10 cwt (½ ton), registered October 1948.

A 1952 Jowett Bradford Javelin van.

Jowett ice-cream van in Liverpool.

Jowett Bradford 1947 pick-up in Uruguay.

The last van off the production line in 1952.

THE SCOTT MOTORCYCLE COMPANY

The Scott Motorcycle Company was founded by Alfred Angas Scott in 1908 as the Scott Engineering Company and was owned by Scott Motors (Saltaire) Ltd, Shipley. Scott motorcycles were still being made up to 1978. Perfecting the two-stroke motorcycle engine was Scott's ambition. His early experiments with a two-stroke were in a motorboat. His first attempt on a motorcycle was when he fitted an engine he had designed to a Premier bicycle in 1901. He had already patented an early form of calliper brakes in 1897, a fully triangulated frame, and rotary induction valves. He invented the kick-start. A vertical twin two-stroke engine came in 1908 featuring a 450cc two-stroke twin-cylinder water-cooled engine. The first few machines were produced by Jowett in 1908; not long after he set up as a manufacturer at the Mornington Works in Grosvenor Road, Bradford.

Here is the general layout of the Scott motorcycle taken from the patent GB190816564 (1908). The Scott motorcycle layout was novel at the time and has many features still used today: 'The present invention relates to improvements in open frame motor cycles, and has for its object to provide a motor cycle with a very low centre of gravity.'

The central fuel tank, mounted low down, is still found on the latest racing motorcycles, the step through frame is found on scooters and commuter machines, the water-cooled two-stroke twin-cylinder engine (subject to a separate patent) was smooth and powerful, and the bike won hill climbs and races to the point where the governing body had to handicap it to allow other makes a chance.

Scott's machines were top of the range and marketed as a 'wheeled horse for the Edwardian Gentleman'. Scott motorcycles were so powerful that they often easily beat four-stroke motorcycles of the same capacity. The First World War saw a sizeable government contract; they were to produce motorcycle and sidecar-based mobile machine-gun batteries with

Scott 550 from 1913, Museo del Motociclo di Rimini.

eighteen machines being sent to the front for testing at the end of 1914. These machine-gun units each comprised three Scott 552cc machines, one with the Vickers gun, one carrying ammunition, and one as a spare.

Scott left the company in 1915 and formed the Scott Autocar Company in Bradford. The aim here was to make a civilian version of his proposed military three-wheel motorcycle/car hybrid. It was to be called the Sociable. Post-war production resumed with the 532cc Standard Tourer and in 1922 the Squirrel, the firm's first sporting model. In 1946 Scott relaunched the Scott Flying Squirrel, but to disappointing sales.

THE BRADFORD TECHNICAL COLLEGE

The Bradford Technical College (1882–1956) was established to cater for the educational needs of the city's textile industries workers. It developed into what is now the University of Bradford.

A big Bradford engineering wheel

The motor car engineering laboratory. This and the image below are taken from an album of photographs that are part of the Bradford Technical College Archive. The album was compiled for the 1911 opening of a new textile department at Bradford Technical College.

The wool-scouring and drying room in the new Textile Block.

LEEDS BRADFORD AIRPORT

The airport that is now Leeds Bradford Airport opened as the Leeds and Bradford Municipal Aerodrome, Yeadon Aerodrome, on 17 October 1931 and was operated by the Yorkshire Aeroplane Club for Leeds and Bradford Corporations. It is 6 miles north of the city. Scheduled flights began in 1935 with a service by North Eastern Airways from London, from Heston Aerodrome to Newcastle-upon-Tyne at Cramlington, later extended to Edinburgh's Turnhouse. Civil aviation was, of course, suspended in 1939.

Avro built a new factory to produce military aircraft just to the north of the aerodrome. Around 5,515 aircraft were produced and delivered from Yeadon during the war including Ansons (over 4,500), Bristol Blenheims (250), Lancasters (695), Yorks (45) and Lincolns (25).

Two new runways, taxiways and extra hangars made Yeadon an important site for military aircraft test flying. The Avro factory was camouflaged, replicating the original field pattern – apparently carried out by people in the film industry – and had dummy cows placed on the roof of the factory to fool German airmen into thinking that it was just a field of cattle beneath them. There were also imitation farm buildings, stone walls and a duck pond placed around the factory. Hedges and bushes made out of fabric were periodically changed to match the changing colours of the seasons. Dummy animals were moved around daily to mimic activity. It all obviously worked because enemy bombers never detected the factory.

At its height during the war there were more than 17,500 people employed at Avro Yeadon. It was one of twenty-six 'shadow factories', and also the largest in Europe with a site of around 34 acres. The factory operated on a 24/7 basis with sixty-nine hours a week working three days followed by three nights. Many of the workers were female – local girls supplemented by large numbers bussed in from all over West Yorkshire. The Ministry of Aircraft Production (MAP) built temporary homes or provided accommodation – for example, on the Westfield Estate in Yeadon and Greenbanks at Horsforth – for workers who lived at a distance from the Avro assembly plant.

British shadow factories came about from the government Shadow Scheme of 1935 in an attempt to meet the urgent need for aircraft using technology from the motor industry. The term 'shadow' has nothing to do with secrecy, but describes the skilled motor industry staff shadowing their own motor industry operations.

The 609 (West Riding) Squadron was formed and based at RAF Yeadon from 10 February 1936 until 27 August 1939 as a day-bomber unit of the Auxiliary Air Force. It was then posted to Catterick. The squadron came back in 1946 with Mosquito MK XXX aircraft. It took receipt of Hawker Hart light bombers in June 1936, soon replaced in December 1937 by Hawker Hinds before the squadron was redesignated a fighter unit on 8 December 1938. There were no fighters, though, until the arrival of Spitfire Mk1s at the end of August 1939, on the eve of the war. The squadron was still staffed by part-time civilians. Fairey Battle light bombers were used as training aircraft to convert pilots from the fixed undercarriage biplane Hinds to the Spitfire with its retractable undercarriage.

After defensive duties in the north, 609 Squadron moved to RAF Northolt in May 1940 and patrolled over Dunkirk as part of Operation Dynamo to cover the evacuation of the BEF.

Around this period, one third of the squadron's pilots were lost over a period of three days. When 609 Squadron decamped to Catterick, Yeadon became a flying training school, bomber maintenance unit, and a scatter airfield. In January 1942 it was transferred to the Ministry of Aircraft Production. Avro then built their shadow factory. It was also used by Hawker Aircraft for development work on its Tornado design.

Leeds Bradford Airport today.

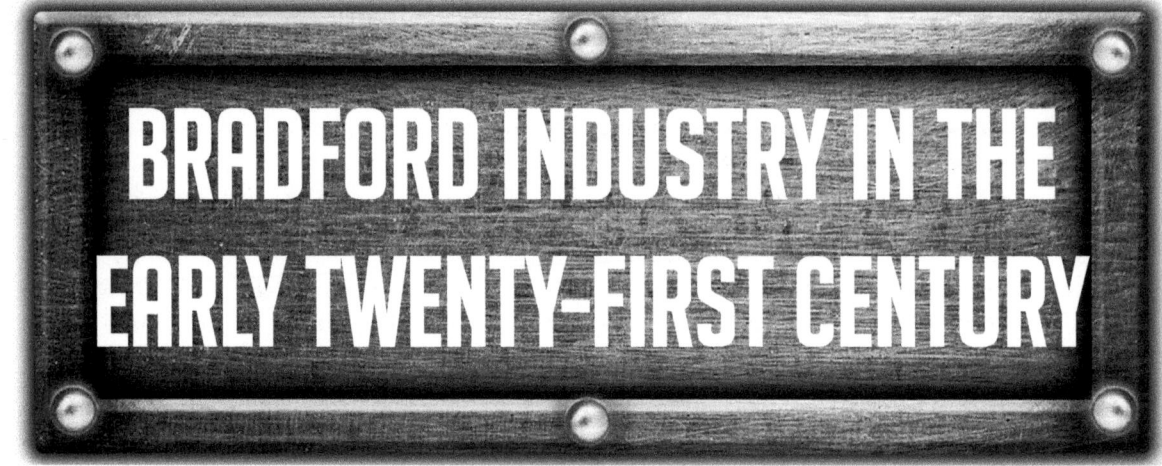

BRADFORD INDUSTRY IN THE EARLY TWENTY-FIRST CENTURY

The textile industry started to decline in the 1920s, causing Bradford to be often cited as an example of deindustrialisation. Nevertheless, Bradford remains one of the North's most commercially and industrially important cities, with information technology, chemicals, engineering, academic and financial sectors replacing Blake's 'dark satanic mills'.

The decline of Bradford's textile industry has permitted a new age of innovative industry in the early twenty-first century. As of 2017, the following companies and organisations had their headquarters in Bradford:

BASF UK subsidiary of the German company in Cleckheaton Road, Low Moor. In 2016 a new world-scale bio-acrylamide (BioACM) production facility was opened at BASF's site in Bradford. It is one of the UK's largest chemical manufacturing facilities, employing around 600 people. Bradford is one of the largest and most productive single-site chemical plants in the UK. The annual output of the site is over 250,000 tonnes, of which 84 per cent is exported. It all started with Allied Colloids over fifty years ago. In 1997, it was acquired by Ciba, and in 2008 by BASF.

British Wool Marketing Board operates the central marketing system for UK fleece wool. Established in 1950, it is the only organisation in the world that collects, grades, sells and promotes fleece wool and is the only remaining agricultural commodity board in the UK.

Damart UK subsidiary of the French company.

Farmers Boy Meat subsidiary of Morrisons plc.

Grattan plc The mail order catalogue company was founded in 1912 by John Enrico Fattorini in Bradford as a result of from a falling out with his cousin when they worked at Empire Stores. Today Grattan has 2,600 employees.

Greenwoods Retailer and mail order of men's clothing, Greenwoods was founded by Willie Greenwood in 1860 as a hatter's shop. At its zenith in the 1990s there were around 200 branches. In 2009, Greenwoods entered administration. Before this Greenwoods had a turnover of £25.9 million and employed 579 people. Greenwoods were headquartered in Albion Mills, Greengates, Bradford, but have now moved to newly built premises on the Shipley Airedale Road.

Hallmark Cards UK subsidiary of this American company.

Kashmir Crown Bakeries Asian food company.

Morrisons This supermarket giant started life in 1899 as an egg and butter merchant in Rawson Market.

Mumtaz Prestigious Asian restaurant chain and food company.

Pace Micro Technology are a set top box developer.

Safestyle UK The UK's largest independent provider of PVC double-glazed windows.

Seabrook Potato Crisps

Telegraph & Argus Bradford's daily newspaper, now printed early morning in Oldham six times a week. The current editor, since 1992, is Perry Austin-Clarke, now also the editor of *The Press* at York, where he spends most of his time. *The Argus Weekly* was based in Argus Chambers in Britannia House over a century ago. *The Yorkshire Evening Argus* and the *Bradford Daily Telegraph* newspapers later merged to form the *Bradford Telegraph & Argus*, which has occupied its present building, the former Milligan and Forbes Warehouse, for decades. 'Bradford' was dropped from the title in the 1930s, when the paper's circulation area spread across much of West Yorkshire. At one time it had branches in nine towns across the region, as well as an office in Morecambe, the retirement seaside town of choice for many Bradford people. At its height the paper's daily sales exceeded 130,000. It is now less than 16,000. Much of the advertising copy is typeset in India.

Yorkshire Building Society The Yorkshire Building Society is the third largest building society in the UK. The Huddersfield Equitable Permanent Benefit Building Society was founded in Huddersfield in 1864. Through expansion and mergers, predominantly with the Bradford Permanent Building Society in 1975, it has evolved into the Yorkshire Building Society. The current name came into use in 1982 following the merger of the Huddersfield & Bradford Building Society and the West Yorkshire Building Society.

Yorkshire Water

The days of the paperboy and girl are numbered – and they seem to know it from their expressions.

Jowett Bradford van in *Bradford Telegraph and Argus* livery. (Photograph by Linda Spashett)